CONTENTS

INTERVIEW: KERSTEN GEERS AND NINA RAPPAPORT

The following discussion between Kersten Geers—who with David Van Severen, founded OFFICE in 2002—and Nina Rappaport was conducted at the start of the semester and focused on practice and teaching.

Nina Rappaport Your office in Brussels has greatly expanded in the past few years. How did you begin the firm with David Van Severen, and what initially brought you together?

Kersten Geers We both share a fascination with Los Angeles, something we realized on a trip to that city together in the late 1990s. A few years later, we made a very small project: a mirror-glass room for a notary office. This project became an early manifesto. In the following years, a few competitions for a border crossing and a new city in South Korea helped us to further define what we thought architecture should be about.

NR Recently, you and David have been focusing on the idea of "architecture without content." One interpretation might be that you are looking to basic shelter, or the idea of the primitive hut, to construct buildings. But you are also making places with inspirational spatial qualities. How do you address this desire to design spaces while keeping a focus on the basics?

KG The basics and making good spaces are not in conflict. From our very first project, David and I have been trying to find out what the basic tools are that one has as an architect, not just for ourselves but also for the architectural community. I think you cannot ignore that context. When we started our practice, OFFICE, in the early 2000s, we were upset with what surrounded us. It was all very diagrammatic, and very simple schemes were sold as buildings. But as representations of a schematic idea, these buildings often also presented solutions to problems.

NR What led you to this stripped-down approach to designing buildings in an era of overproduction?

KG There were two things we wanted to address from the very beginning: architecture doesn't solve anything, and architecture always stands in the way. And, of course, these were provocative positions. It's simply a mistake to make a rendering of a transparent volume and claim that it would make your building more democratic. We tried to go back to simpler ideas, because for two thousand years, architecture was what it was, and then, all of a sudden, with the echo of late Modernism it was something that was solved in a functionalist,

Architecture without Content 19: ALMOST CLASSICISM

Kersten Geers

YALE SCHOOL OF ARCHITECTURE

FUTURE REAL

THE LOUIS I. KAHN VISITING ASSISTANT PROFESSORSHIP

OFFICE 15, Border Crossing, 2005, OFFICE Kersten Geers David Van Severen

diagrammatic way. Then, with the idea being embraced by the media, everything was more simplistic.

NR You also say that you're not functionalists, in terms of the program driving the form of the building, and that you allow for the inhabitant to create the spaces they need. Is this achieved in your idea of the "big box," where you provide a shell in which people can do what they want spatially?

KG That's right. Again, we think this is something that architecture has always done, not just two thousand years ago but also two hundred years ago. If you look at Brussels, Paris, or anywhere else, the big houses had plans that had been endlessly transformed, whereas the architecture stayed the same. It was a big deal for us to understand that you don't have to define spaces functionally but, rather, you can engage sequences, relationships, sizes, proportions, and perhaps materialization. That a project can be a big space—a set of rooms with very peculiar spatial relationships between one and the other, through the perimeter, through the corridor, through the corner.

NR So, with that approach, you try to show how, as you say, "architecture is architecture"? Many of your first projects were like artworks or set pieces.

KG We cannot avoid knowing where we are today as cultural producers. As such, you are always somehow making only a representation of what you want to make. There is an aspect of fiction to doing what you want to do because the world simply does not function that way. Referring to artworks, you are right in the sense that every piece of architecture that you make holds the narrative of what it would like to be.

NR Because it changes over time.

KG Yes, but I would even argue something that wasn't that clear to me ten years ago: in the Renaissance—with Bramante, for example—you see architecture that is trying to represent what it would like to achieve. It accumulates elements of what it sees as its main reference but is totally aware of the fact that it is unable to make what it would like to make. There is the idea of ideal architecture, and there is the idea of the world—and somehow these two things don't fit together.

NR Once you've delivered architecture to the world, it becomes its own thing. The architect has to let go of the design.

KG It is also the experiential side of architecture. There is a certain fiction involved, despite all your good intentions, in the balance between what it would like to be and what it is. And it finds a solution that is neither one nor the other.

NR You and David seem to be able to put your projects forward while maintaining a critical distance.

KG Yes, and I think a common problem of architects in general is that they can be utterly uncritical.

NR Do you say that because only 20 percent of a design project becomes architecture? Architecture is built with a context, a client, a site, a budget, and a series of zoning and building regulations—an entire set of parameters—but this doesn't seem to bother you.

KG I think that is the beautiful thing about architecture: the moment you acknowledge the limitations, you can start to design quite a bit. I see this on two levels. If you work on a specific house for a very particular client, you can still design a lot. But you cannot design the client's life, so you organize the space in a certain way. You are very rigid as to how the architecture is translated into matter, but somehow you convince these people that a house can be used in many different ways. Maybe they don't know if they want one room or two rooms, one kid or two kids, and in twenty-five years the kids are gone. These things are fundamental in architecture. Increasingly, we are designing more industrial buildings for which the envelope is often the only place where there is room to design.

NR It must be interesting to work in the area between high-end design and non-design, which few architects are

OFFICE 155 Housing Block, Jette, 2016, OFFICE Kersten Geers David Van Severen

engaging. How are you able to design a generic shed with architectural intrigue or specificity, like your Arbor Drying Hall, in Herselt?

KG That is very much what we try to do. It isn't easy, but we try to figure out the functions in the existing envelope. When we did the Arbor Drying Hall, the client already had a design in a standard box. It was a huge tree nursery that was fulfilling big urban plans—for example, they might need five thousand of a certain kind of tree at once. They transport the trees in a truck, but they need to dry them first so they don't rot. The company had a standard box, with a pitched roof and a couple of grills for the wind to pass through. Our landscape designer, Bas Smets, with whom we often collaborate, convinced the client that it was a good moment to do architecture. And the architect loved architecture, so he allowed for 10 percent additional construction costs for "good" architecture, which is not very much. We had to persuade him to use corrugated, perforated metal-panel façades, rather than wood, because he couldn't afford

OFFICE 176 Campus RTS, 2014-x , OFFICE Kersten Geers David Van Severen

the wood anyway. We peeled off the standard layers of the box because the wind had to blow through it, and we made the building a bit too big so that the rain and the wind could enter. So, we built it for only 10 percent more money. The material was the same price; the difference was that it was highly technical and precise, like furniture design.

NR As you cultivate new scales of work in housing developments, can you still focus on this precision and pragmatism? How will you be able to stay grounded within an economy of means?

KG It is a big challenge for us. There is a danger that we could start to repeat ourselves. But we have developed an interest in collective housing because it is possible to define individual concepts and fields of inquiry. In collective housing, there is a place where you have to do something because you are building a city with it. Of course, this is the latent presence

of Colin Rowe. Since we are always lost between Koolhaas and Kollhoff, we thought it was time to find our own agenda in the house by providing a rigid framework that the residents have to negotiate.

NR How did you win the competition for your new project for Radio Télévision Suisse [RTS] on the École Polytechnique Fédérale de Lausanne [EPFL] campus in Lausanne, adjacent to SANAA's student center?

KG We were invited to be part of a competition. In the first phase, we had to send a sketch plus a micro-portfolio. Then, we were selected along with seven others. We got very lucky. It was a unique competition formula. They gave us six months, with three presentations in total, one every two months. After two months, we presented a general idea; after four months, we had to show how we responded to their feedback.

NR It's like a studio review process.

KG It was. And we were, by far, the youngest team involved. I think we had a chance because of that. The jury said it was clear that we were listening to their comments and were professional. I had the impression that it also had a lot to do with the 20 percent argument. We were very reduced in terms of what we wanted to define; we essentially designed a complex of five boxes. We understood the RTS building, which is a building for radio and television production, as a big, open workspace, as a continuous interior carried by four big boxes. The volumes are structural; they carry the field of the production landscape. They contain either big halls for recording studios or a set of floors for offices. With these spatial types, many decisions were made, but, at the same time, the precise use and infill was kept open and flexible.

NR What other projects are you working on that are currently informing your architectural concepts or ideology?

KG I think, in some respects, designing the RTS building has had a major impact on the way we think we can design the architectural form in radical disconnection to its content—real "architecture without content," so to speak. The three years in which we have been developing the building since winning the competition showed us the extreme liberty that results from the definition of the two spatial conditions of the building: the box and the field. In the process toward final design, the four boxes have already contained many things—studios, garages, a media center, offices—without somehow loosing their spatial and architectural definition. The field has been designed and organized by the existence of the boxes. The main quality, in terms of light, space, and air, is always guaranteed by the sheds. Up to today, that is still the case, but an area of offices for media production went through various phases of radical redesign. Yet, I feel I can safely state that the overall idea of the RTS media building is now, three years after the initial pitch, still very much there. Its urban stance toward the university campus of EPFL and Université de Lausanne [UNIL] is still valid and important. The ensemble of its different spatial types is still productive. So, perhaps, the particularity of this media building or, maybe better, the ambiguity of its ever-evolving content allowed us to fundamentally research and test many themes we so much caress in architecture without content.

On more recent projects, like a recently won housing complex in Brussels or a crematorium in Oostende, we further developed subthemes we discussed earlier but, of course, only fragmentarily. The projects are simpler, so the complexity is found in other challenges. The housing scheme proposed to house the units in three small towers and a lower strip or bar-like building. The bar makes some kind of background that the towers use to seek a more metropolitan relationship with the city and the canal. The plan is almost secondary. The architecture is made with the simple volumes and the thickness of the façade.

The crematorium is part of the family of utilitarian boxes. At the same time, it is

OFFICE 117 Drying Hall, 2011–2013, OFFICE Kersten Geers David Van Severen

a decisively public building, albeit for a specific public. Here, I feel the big challenge is to make a building that is as much representative as machine. The box-like building we developed with the artist Richard Venlet looks like a slightly tilted, oversize table. The top of the table works as fifth façade—as a nature *morte* or still life—with the ambition to represent the unrepresentable, which is a key issue for a building so symbolic yet so ambiguous as a crematorium. So, here, perhaps, the box finally manages to fully fullfill its "public function."

NR Of great interest to many is your drawing technique, which could be considered very prescriptive, along with your use of collage and rendering. Who were the main influences, besides Superstudio, on your technique?

KG In the early 2000s, we were influenced by Superstudio's perspectives and plans and the idea of composing. It felt like a fascinating discovery. We were also influenced by how David Hockney paintings and Bas Princen photographs are composed, as well as by our time in Los Angeles. We don't have computer-rendering programs in the office, so we only make two or three views with a hierarchical system—and the rest you don't know. We have to decide what is important. For the early competition involving the border crossing in Mexico, two perspectives had to tell the entire story.

NR How does that translate into your teaching methods?

KG We try to make students understand this simple technique, but they try to mimic a certain aesthetic. They use SketchUp. Instead, we ask them to compose the image so they understand how to draw. I don't like it when students try to emulate a professor's architecture. At the same time, of course, what you share as a teacher is a way of looking. I've been teaching with Andrea Zanderigo for the past eight years, and we share a total love for architecture. We like to look at buildings and understand them. We feel that this generation of students doesn't really look at buildings—they Google things.

NR What do you like to teach in the U.S.?

KG When I teach in the States, I try to salvage the possibility of doing architecture in a world that isn't ready for it. There is architecture for the city, and there is architecture for the countryside. But is that really true? In the studios we did recently in Europe, we worked around the idea of "the even covered field," a condition in which the distinction between city and landscape is annihilated but hierarchies are very much needed. Perhaps, in the U.S., distinctions between field and city are bigger, but the challenges are similar. Also, we have to reintroduce something to share, a commons, which is something that I believe is central to cultural production and to architecture. It defines its *raison d'être*. At Yale, we worked on "the village." The argument is that, perhaps, with a mild Classicism, it is possible to awaken Venturi's dream of North Canton, Ohio, by way of Kevin Roche's and Scamozzi's simplified architecture, which a precise architecture might have the ability to create. It's a gamble, but it was worth it.

NR It seems that you are on a mission with this process.

KG What we try to regain, as architects, is the ability to decide about the hierarchies of the building—that you can achieve maximum effect with minimal things. You can focus on the role of the joint, the plan, the section, the perspective. Ultimately, we want to make people understand that architecture is about taking responsibility, about intentionality.

I feel that, in hindsight, that is also what the students took. It was never intended that way, but the "commons" studio also became, in many ways, a studio that wanted to depict a certain side of the United States of America. I feel all the students were very aware of that. The village of our studio became a place where certain desires, perhaps certain frustrations about the area in which many of the students grew up, could be attacked, could be compensated. Thus, we ended up making co-op complexes in Iowa and micro-islands in Ohio. To be honest, I would have never expected that visiting Rossi and Scamozzi in the long lost fields of Italy could result in such an expression of—by the way, very much needed—American neo-romanticism. I think all is not yet lost.

OFFICE 35 Ceuta, 2007, OFFICE Kersten Geers David Van Severen

STUDIO DESCRIPTION

This studio was conceived during the long, confusing run-up to the 2016 presidential election, the troubling aftermath of which still resonates today. Ideological politics aside, probably one of the most fundamental insights during the campaign was a total lack of middle ground. The city was (again) opposed to the countryside, the coast to the inland, the educated to the non-educated, the black to the white, the women to the men. We witnessed an impasse not easy to overcome and, in many ways, impossible to tackle with architecture or planning. There has been a lot of writing on the atomization of what used to be our society due to the new and now ubiquitous means of communication at our disposal. Virtual technology platforms seem to allow for any rant and opinion to surface on the internet, without real consequences. A lack of immediate accountability results in fake claims and suppressed frustration. In the ephemeral world of internet bleeps where anyone can say anything without ever confronting the recipient of the message, architecture is a lost figure.

My fascination with the United States goes back a long way. Foremost, as a place, it seems to be an experiment in scale, numbers, and size, which, although not unique, makes this country most recognizable and easy to relate to us, as Europeans, as compared to say, China. Where everything is roughly the same, the dimensions make the difference. Does a bigger country bring bigger problems? With only a handful of megacities at the coastline and a dozen or so fantastic stretches of no-man's-land national parks, this country is a perfect representation of the "even covered field." Fragments of villages, agricultural communities, and postindustrial towns litter an undefined landscape. These villages have perhaps always emulated another idea of a village, imported from another continent, with another intensity. Despite the differences, at a certain point in time the villages were efficient in their centrality, carefully planned, and unconditionally shared. If the American mind-set has always been one of collective restraint, with a minimum of shared goals organized as micro-points of common engagement in an otherwise alien and malleable landscape, these small centers provided a point of gravity.

Alienated, third-generation farmers surf the internet to meet the only person they talk to all day. Lower-middle-class kids of postindustrial workers meet in Taco Bell's parking lot. Post offices are gone, city halls have lost their significance, schools have become "protected areas," and libraries are being closed. Here lies the physical drama of Mittel Amerika. The current political turmoil is deeply connected to the way middle America lives, both physically and virtually. Sadly, it represents the conditions of "the even covered field" in our Western world. Nothing is connected, yet everything is deeply related. Without being nostalgic, we should try to find out how we, as architects and planners, can still offer alternatives to this malaise. Can we revive the village as a place of shared values, even if that means having to rethink its very DNA? Or is the village really dead?

It was not difficult to convince the students of this studio to engage in exactly that task. All of them but one grew up in the Midwest, in the suburban middle class, in the field. All of them met in Taco Bells and McDonalds, hung around the malls and parking lots, felt estranged surrounded by the agricultural fields. Thus, searching for case studies turned out to be rather easy for the studio as more than half the students spent part of their lives either in Iowa or Ohio. Both states belong to the Mississippi River watershed. Both states play a disproportionally important role in election primaries. Both states present the current state of the field in its two extremes. The loneliness of Iowa and the loneliness of Ohio could not be more different. Ohio is a textbook example of postindustrial suburbia: a post-Hoover, post-village realm where one finds islands of slightly denser programs in a sea of nothingness. Everything in the post-village realm is there, and everything works somehow. But in the landscape of highways, streets, and single-family houses, even a small densification manages to disappear. Iowa is a farmers' paradise gone berserk. It is a meticulously planned division of land and manpower that developed in a universe of agricultural solitude. Due to this extreme lack of interaction at every level, knowledge as a building block of society quickly vanishes. Both states thus create a backdrop for an experiment in architectural form as some kind of memory stone; a project that acts as an obstruction against the fast erosion of these vulnerable landscapes.

In the case of Iowa, the Yale studio project became one of an atomized cooperation. Different incarnations of co-op complexes defined alternative village structures within a landscape dominated by work. Common space and tools were linked to common knowledge, trade, and education. Thus, each of the six studio projects presents a center of collected tools as a contemporary village center. In all cases, these complexes were developed in ignorance of existing points of concentration. So, agriculture is reinterpreted not as the destroyer of civic society but as its potential savior. Ohio is in many ways a situation more familiar to us, as architects, but perhaps for that reason one without clear remedy. Since work and habitation here have long lost their connection to the land and the landscape, the argument was developed that one could force some kind of artificial centrality only through densification. A landscape already defined by almost invisible islands was made more readable through simple exaggeration. Each of the projects intensified an activity already present in the field in an attempt to make the field a considerable player in the endlessly repetitive landscape. Elderly housing became a low building with territorial ambitions, a drive-in church became an accumulation of forms (and belief systems), shabby motel infrastructure had castle-like ambitions, and sport was able to make a village of unparalleled dimensions. Together with markets, offices, and parking lots, these interventions present the atomized status quo of the village that is gone, but perhaps they are still able to show the size of the field and compete with the dimensions of the landscape.

If we could make one conclusion out of this seemingly impossible task to salvage the village in an urbanized landscape that has far outgrown its initial dimensions, it is perhaps that, in "the even covered field," the village itself expanded to the dimensions of the landscape. The dichotomy between the small, familiar entity and that gigantic other no longer exists, and any nostalgic attempt to re-enact it is bound to fail. Surprisingly, however, any big intervention with a minimum of shared ambition seems to weather well in a territory that is, ultimately, all the same. Size matters. The new village does not need total consensus, but consensus of a few might be more than enough. As it appears, the middle can also be atomized. Reimagining the contemporary village center as a center of collected tools, can this micro middle ground act as a stepping-stone to another collective responsibility? Politics can't wait.

STUDIO BRIEF

Argument

This is the nineteenth incarnation of our Architecture without Content series. The series originally started as an investigation into the "big box" but quickly turned into a discourse on architecture reduced to the perimeter. Over time, this focus has shifted. As the scale was the primary preoccupation, big boxes were supposed to have certain qualities due to their sheer size. Gradually, scale and strategic location became our obsessions, turning our original concerns—about an architecture "so big that it can contain anything"—into architectures that are able to organize the landscape due to their precise proportions and intricate positioning.

Central to this investigation is the axiom that our contemporary society transformed the totality of the environment into an "even covered field," a continuous interior where No-Stop City is fully realized, though in a form that makes it mostly unrecognizable (the consequence of one hundred years of the Modernist project). As our preoccupations changed, so did the titles of our respective studios. With the studios "Roman Architecture" and "Metropolitan Architecture," the territory entered the discourse. The original inspiration for the "big box"—the States—was carefully kept at a distance, only to be introduced in an indirect way. Initially, a few semesters ago, we reconnected to the scale issue. "Boxes for America" investigated the limits of size in the most literal sense. Through a careful study of Palladio's Veneto villas, we first tried to update any Roman architecture and then transplanted it.

"Neon Palladian" is to be seen as a precise but rather abstract affair. It did, however, clear ground for a more thorough investigation of the field in the U.S. As long as we considered the "even covered field" in Europe, Roman Classicism seemed the language of choice, because history simply proved us right. In the American countryside, things are laid out rather differently, not least because the differences that exist between the European cities and their countryside, socially and ideologically, are here exacerbated. If the "even covered field" in a European context is a formal fait accompli, perhaps in the States it makes for an ideological projection. Current in all projects of Architecture without Content is the conviction that no architectural project, however formal and autonomous, is able to be relevant without tackling the commons, the shared.

Any project, from box to perimeter, has the commons as a part of its DNA. If we want to tackle the American field, this can be in no way different. Thus, "Almost Classicism" carries this notion in its core. "Almost Classicism" continues where "Neon Palladian" left us. It starts in full conviction that the current

1:5000 Perspective by Charles Kane

1:20 Perspective by Anthony Gagliardi

project on the United States has to focus both on the countryside and on an attempt to reintroduce some kind of commons. We feel the best way to illustrate this is to start where the commons have dissolved in what used to be called "the village." The village is the shared core in the field. This studio wants to develop projects in order to formalize this idea. But how? Perhaps a kind of Classicism Lite or a pragmatic Classicism can show the way.

When, in 1963, Kevin Roche and John Dinkeloo took over Saarinen's practice after the founder's death, they instantly got rid of the complex formal experiments of the immigrant architect. What was the point of this redundant heroism anyway? This decision was not necessarily one of urgency; there was plenty of work, so no compromises had to be made. Rather, it was one of pragmatism—architecture should only be so complex, so heroic, so radical. Type and a certain typological experiment replaced formal heroism. Size replaced monumentality, and interior complexity and refinement replaced exhibitionist exuberance. Was the Roche-Dinkeloo practice of the sixties till the eighties a correction?

Four hundred years earlier, when Vincenzo Scamozzi finished the Villa Rotonda by Palladio in the 1560s, he was also something like a collaborator. In parallel, he was commissioned to work on the Villa Rocca Pisana by the same client of Palladio, leading him to gradually develop a more pedestrian version of the heroic Classicism his master had reinvented. Also, when the same Scamozzi built the "Procuratie" to finish the Piazza San Marco, he got rid of the strange, beautiful, and refined cornice and proportions introduced by Sansovino's library. The building was too big for that, the actual purpose too pragmatic; therefore, a simpler, more utilitarian answer emerged. Is Scamozzi's architecture simply an architecture whose core argument is not to be found in the language but in the structure of the building? Perhaps. Scamozzi certainly redefined the canon of Classicism as a pragmatic and utilitarian set of principles with a maximum effect.

In 1965, Robert Venturi and John Rauch were commissioned to design a city center for North Canton, Ohio. The project was never realized, but it did leave us with a set of coherent buildings that try to define a commons for a small town. This studio, "Almost Classicism," took the challenge of Venturi again but suggested the reading of a possible answer in the axis of Roche-Scamozzi. Thus, we hoped to define a prototypical project for the village in the countryside. The current infrastructure of the American town is in a dismal state. It is urgently in need of update. Complex, often politicized discussions make change and transformation seldom possible. However, we would argue that the benefits for these small communities easily outweigh the relatively modest investment in the commons, which might be able to bring back a sense of hierarchy and—who knows?—a sense of belonging to the American field.

Starting with a set of simple and, perhaps, related buildings that replace the outlived infrastructure of today—city halls, police stations, fire stations, schools—we hope to present a portrait of the village of tomorrow, not as some kind of weird tech dream but, rather, as a few elements to anchor the increasingly pulverized life we live in the new land, once conquered and transformed into the (un)even covered field.

Here, in this book, two tracks are presented: a set of projects in agricultural Iowa that rethink the co-op as a series of small village centers, and another set of projects in postindustrial Ohio, where, in the post-Hoover revival, fragments, and islands are formalized as micro-urban organisms. Are these simple but effective gestures able to turn the tide? In the field that is all the same, a pebble could make the difference. It is purely a matter of precision.

Studio Challenge

The challenge posed to the students was to make a project for a set of village amenities—town house, fire station, police station, school—in search of an updated idea of the commons in a representative part of the Midwest.

Organization

The first part of the studio, "Ancestors (and the Search for a Village)," was dedicated to the study of a selection of architectural "ancestors" that would be used as precedent studies in the later development of projects. Secondly, the studio dedicated its collective effort to "search for a village." In other words, the students were asked to choose the specific location for all the projects, including the state, region, and village. In this part, the studio made a visit to the Roche buildings in Connecticut.

The second part of the studio, "The Village," was a transition from ancestor to project. The studio as a whole made a set of coherent buildings, and the selection had to include four sets of ancestors and two sets of sites. Further, students were asked to consider two central questions in making this set: What makes a set? and what defines a pragmatic whole?

During the second part, the studio trip served as an opportunity to study a series of buildings in Milan and Venice, including schools by Rossi and many buildings by Scamozzi.

In the third part, "Set as a Portrait of the Village," the exemplary building set was developed as a portrait of a village in the United States. The two selected states, Iowa and Ohio, would provide the backdrop for the two subsequent sets of projects. At this point, the students were working individually on their commons proposal. In each case, the argument for one individual proposal and the set of buildings was the same.

Format

The students were required to produce six images at A0 paper sizes (841 x 1189 millimeters) in two rows of three panels. The first panel had to include a perspective from 2,000 meters away and a plan/drawing at 1:2000 meters. The second panel had to include a perspective from 200 meters away and a plan/drawing at 1:200 meters, and, finally, the third panel had to include a perspective from 20 meters away and a plan/drawing at 1:20 meters.

STUDENT WORK

ANDREW STERNAD
MOTEL ISLAND

Ancestor:
Cummins Engine Company Headquarters
(Columbus, Indiana)
Kevin Roche

Motel Island is a full-service, extended-stay hotel located at the edge between an agricultural field and an urban center. The sixty-foot-high hilltop off a highway exit is a typical site for unremarkable buildings, and the hotel takes advantage of the topography to both define the existing cluster of buildings within and reveal its presence from outside.

From a macroeconomic view, this site is exactly where it should be. Hotel agglomerations are commonplace at highway exits across America, located according to regional demand and clustered in order to differentiate subtleties in the chain hotel market. Motel Island has seventy-five single rooms—the approximate amount of rooms of a standard chain hotel—and forty-eight extended-stay suites, with a strip-mall arcade at street level. The hotel rooms face in, toward the existing hotels, while the suites face out, toward the loosely defined town. Across the highway, another linear hotel building implies the completed frame of the hotel cluster. The framing strategy was inspired by an ancestor project, Kevin Roche's Cummins Engine Company Headquarters, in Columbus, Indiana. Like Motel Island, the headquarters magnifies its civic presence with a trellis-like arcade that surrounds a historic structure on the property. Motel Island is an extreme intervention in the suburban landscape with a minimum of architecture. The site is already an accumulation of one type of program—an island—within the sea of suburban sameness and by design, largely hidden from view. The project seeks a unified reading of this group from the surrounding development, while creating a sense of place for the transient, yet ever-present, hotel-guest population.

1.

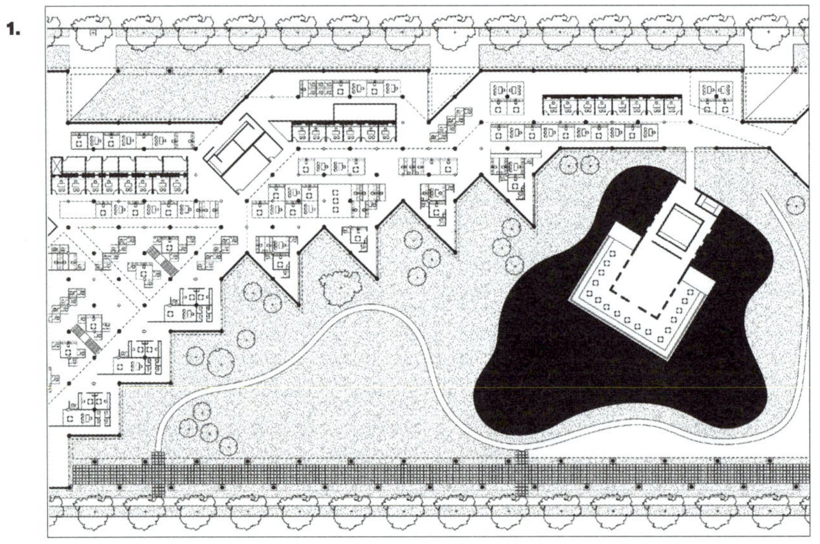

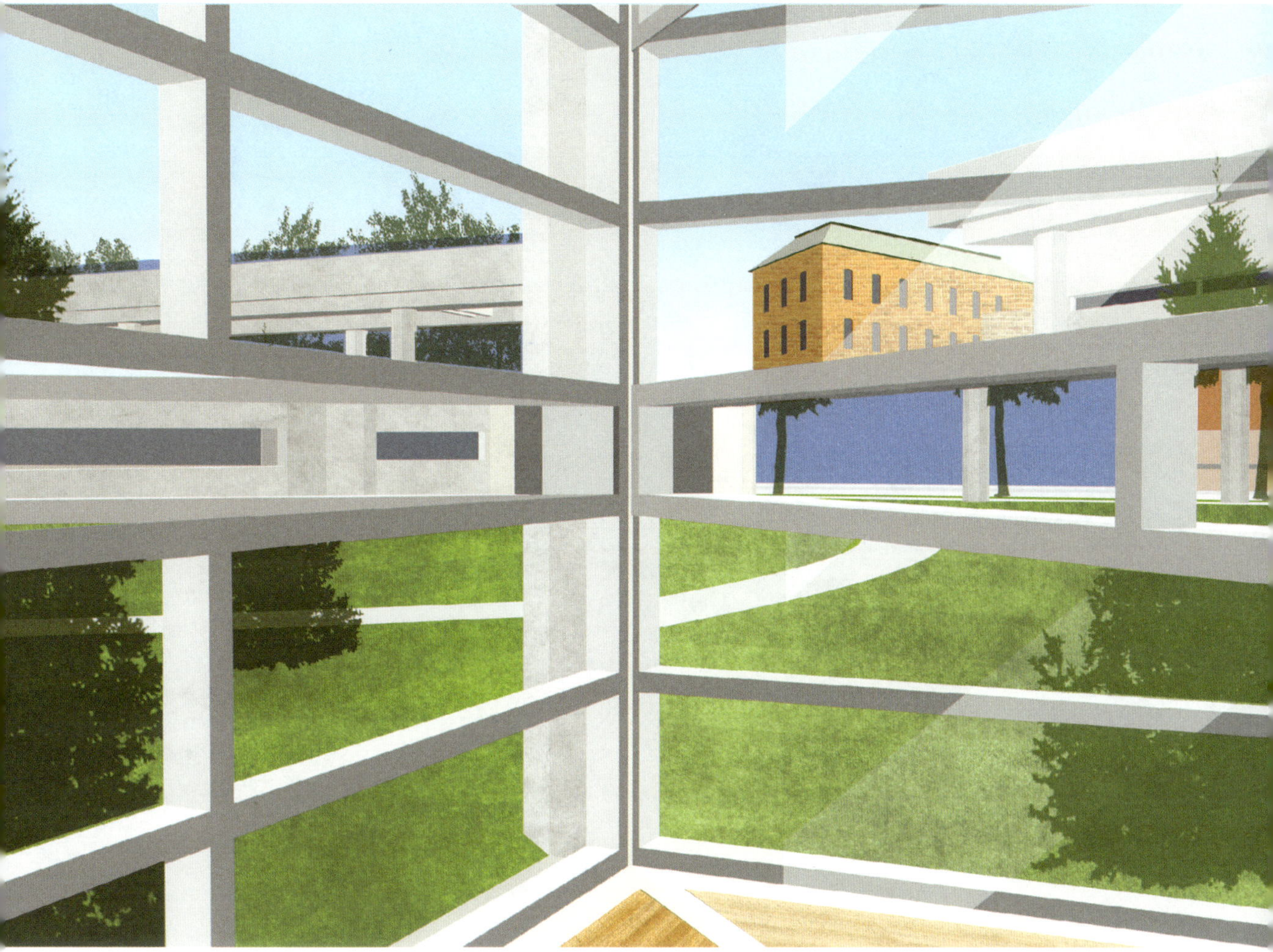

2.

1. Ancestor drawing: Cummins HQ 1:200 Plan
2. Ancestor drawing: Cummins HQ 1:2000 Perspective
3. Ancestor drawing: Cummins HQ 1:200 Perspective

3.

4.

4. Ancestor drawing: Cummins HQ 1:2000 Perspective
5. 1:50 Perspective
6. 1:500 Plan and section

5.

6.

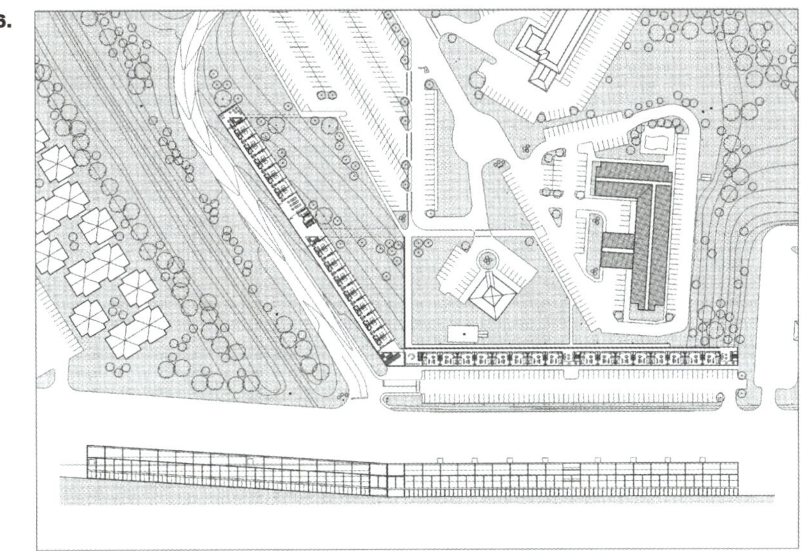

ANTHONY GAGLIARDI ASSISTED-LIVING HOME

Ancestor:
City Hall
(Muggiò, Italy)
Aldo Rossi

Francesco Dal Co stated, "After all, isn't kitsch the ultimate mask of the banal, the sublime of the obvious?" This project argues, in a kitsch manner, that the village has not changed: the suburban commons is family, and that has always existed. One increasingly invisible part of the family is exemplified by the grandparent who gets sent to an assisted-living home. Relegated to a city's borders, these facilities are islands, where their immobile residents are surrounded by everything they need but nothing they can reach. Only one assisted-living home exists in North Canton, Ohio. It is at full capacity, and the state's population of citizens over the age of sixty-five is predicted to increase to over 50 percent from the current 15 percent in the next twenty-years. This project proposes a large-scale assisted-living facility in the form of a fractured square, that frames the eclectic and comprehensive amenities of a suburban intersection and grants visibility to a concealed part of the family.

1.

2.

1. Ancestor drawing: Muggio Town Hall 1:200 Perspective
2. Ancestor drawing: Muggio Town Hall 1:20 Perspective
3. Ancestor drawing: Muggio Town Hall 1:200 Plan

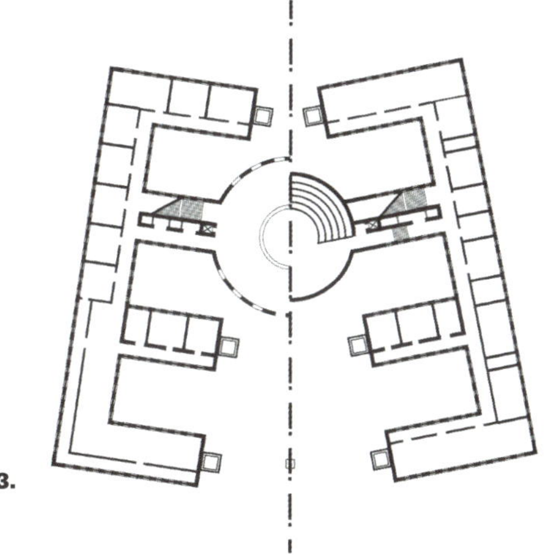

3.

4.

4. 1:50 Perspective
5. 1:50 Plan and section
6. 1:500 Plan
7. 1:500 Perspective

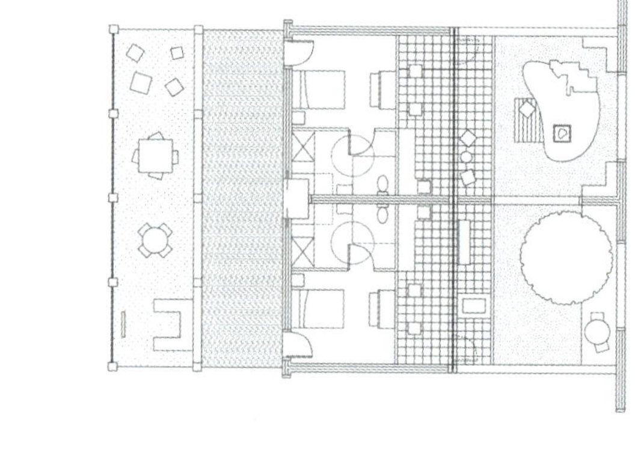

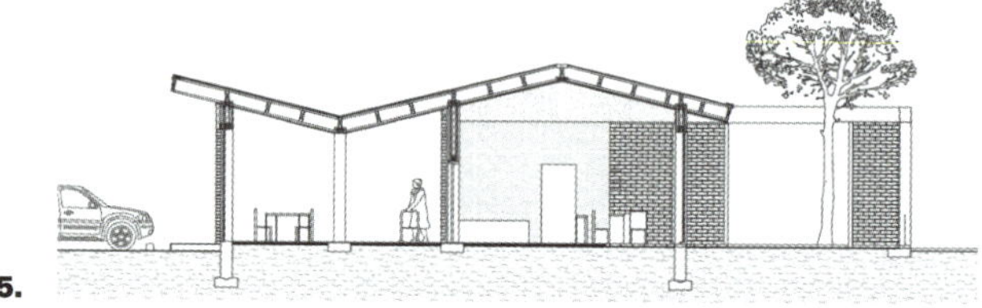

5.

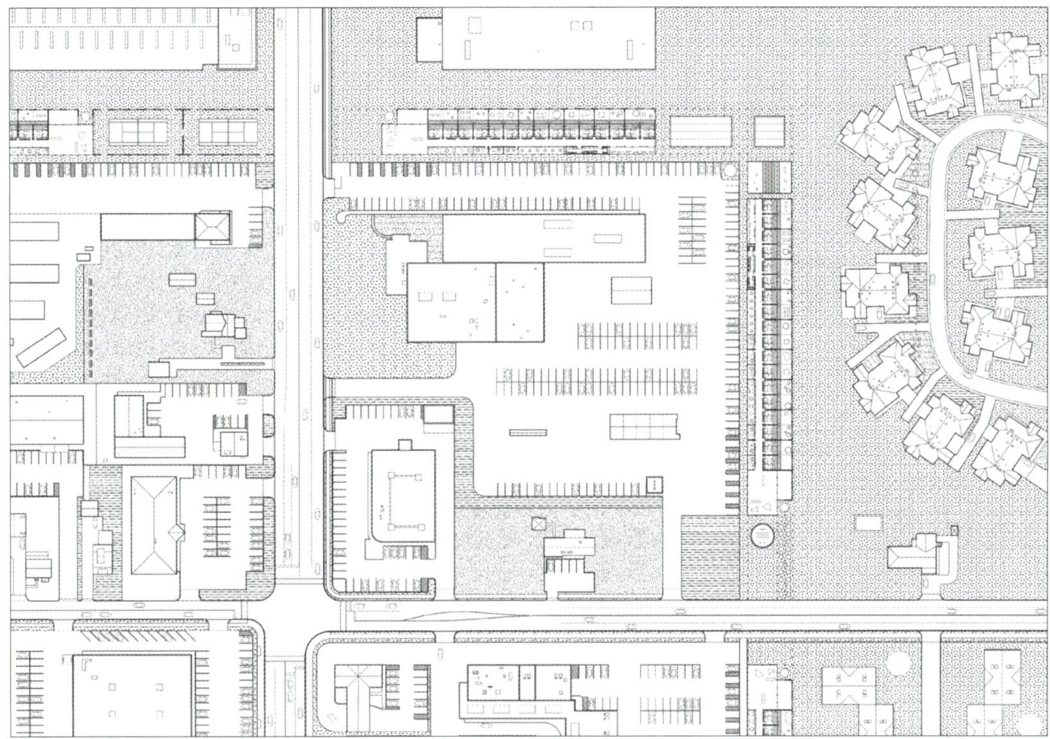

6.

7.

CARL CORNILSEN
AN INDUSTRIAL COMMON

Ancestor:
Rocca Pisana
(Lonigo, Italy)
Vincenzo Scamozzi

North Canton, Ohio lies in an invisible eddy within the sea of international trade, known as a Foreign Trade Zone (FTZ). A manufacturing company that locates in such a zone improves its competitive position. This benefit is normally only available to large corporations.

This proposal seeks to create a window into the American industrial common, by both revealing an invisible aspect and making it available to a wider cross-section of local businesses and startups.

The structural and material design starts from the goal of lightening the building, which had to occupy a very large lot area with an economy of means. Using a long span structure and an envelope with passive ventilation, varying degrees of transparency control heat gain and light during the day while appearing like a lantern at night.

The building's ground floor is organized according to the industrial logic of shipping and receiving. Each five-bay module running from west to east is configurable according to the needs of the tenant. Materials arrive and are stored along the western edge. This storage bay is spanned by a light-weight modular frame system to provide live-work quarters. The open-bay manufacturing floor can accommodate a wide range of industrial assembly such as furniture, electronics, and footwear. Flexible office space sits above an area to store inventory and to package finished goods. The final bay to the east can either be sectioned off as a showroom or become a staging area for finished goods ready to ship.

The result is not a repetition or a copy of the surrounding warehouses, but rather a contemporary building that accommodates new forms of production and the engagement with it.

1.

2.

1. 1:50 Perspective
2. 1:50 Perspective
3. 1:50 Section

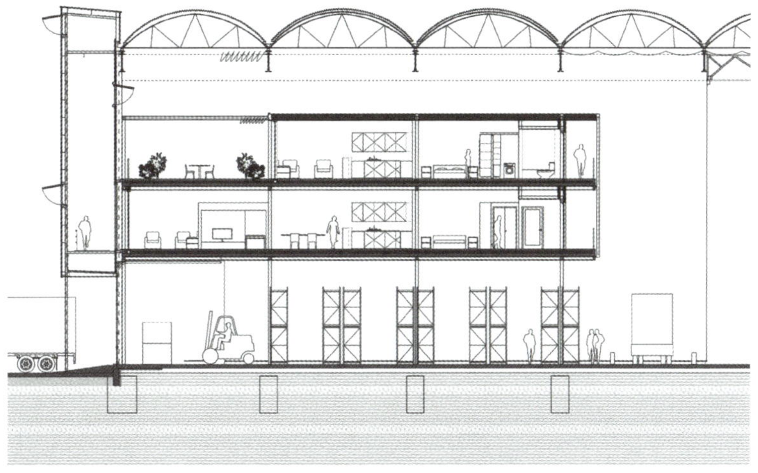

3.

4.

4. Ancestor Drawing 1:5000 Perspective
5. 1:5000 Plan

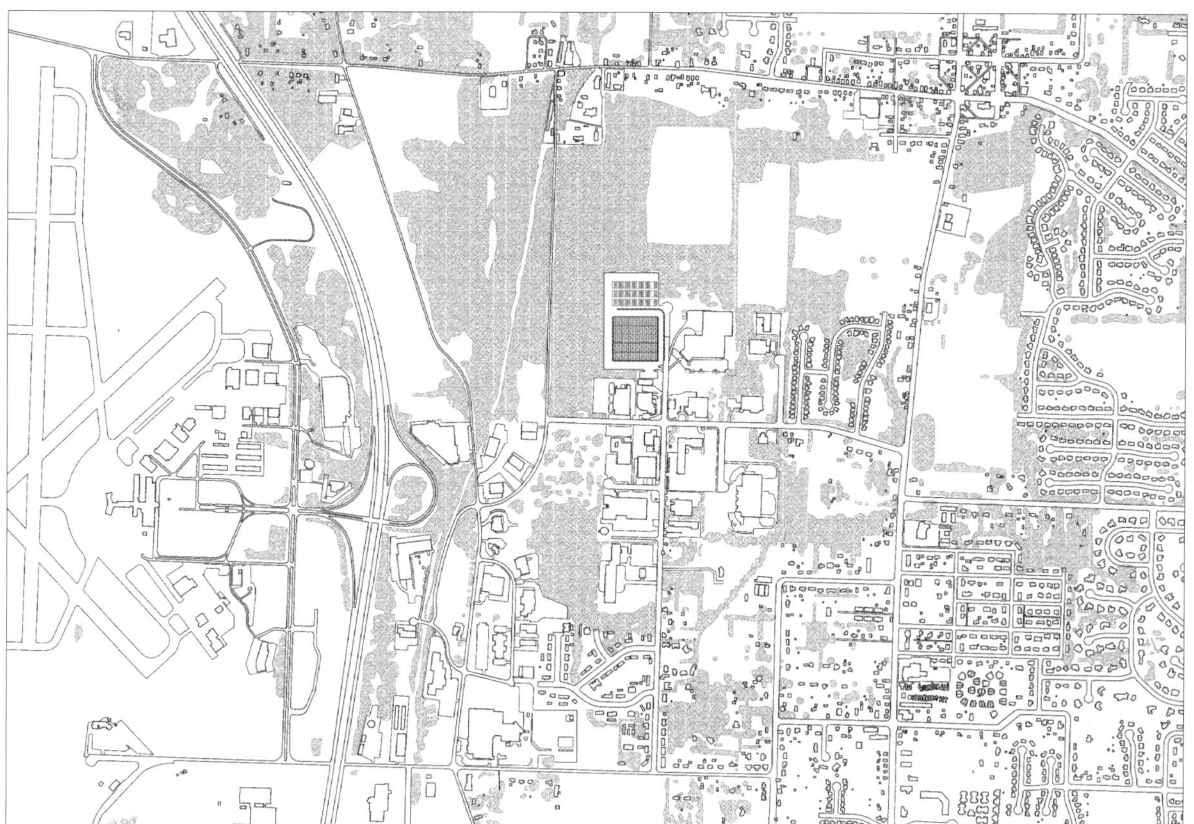

5.

1.

1. Ancestor drawing: Venturi, YMCA 1:200 Perspective
2. Ancestor drawing: Venturi, YMCA 1:2000 Plan
3. 1:500 Plan

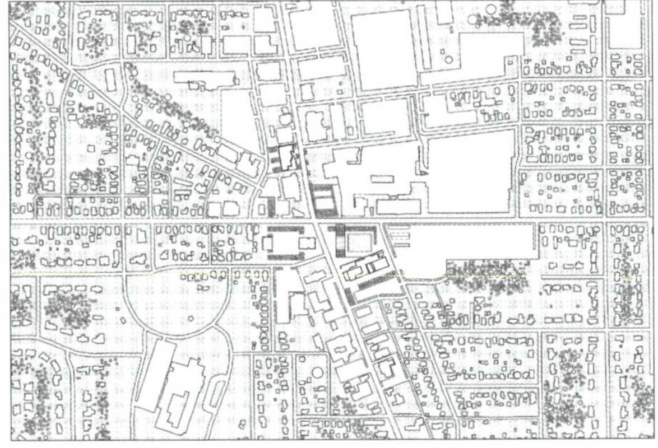

2.

CHARLES ANDERSON KANE SPORTS ISLAND

Ancestor:
YMCA
(North Canton, Ohio)
Robert Venturi

This vast sports complex seeks to capitalize on the suburb's single-use character and amplify it as a means to collect people in a shared space. In order to reach the largest number of people, the project is strategically nestled within a stand of trees and between an airport, highway, and the nebulous boundary between two communities. In today's virtual society, sports offer one of the few activities that require both shared physical space and active interaction. However, playing fields and courts are normally tucked away and left to deteriorate behind schools or community churches. In this project, in order to reach a critical mass, unrelated sports are agglomerated in close proximity and visually linked with a lightly structured roof. With the addition of restaurants and team dormitories, the complex grants the curious visitor one vision of a contemporary village.

3.

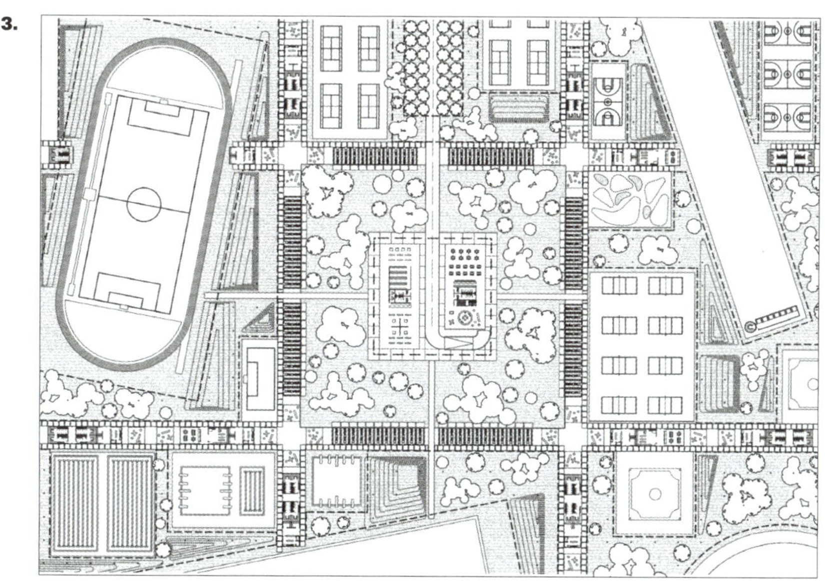

4.

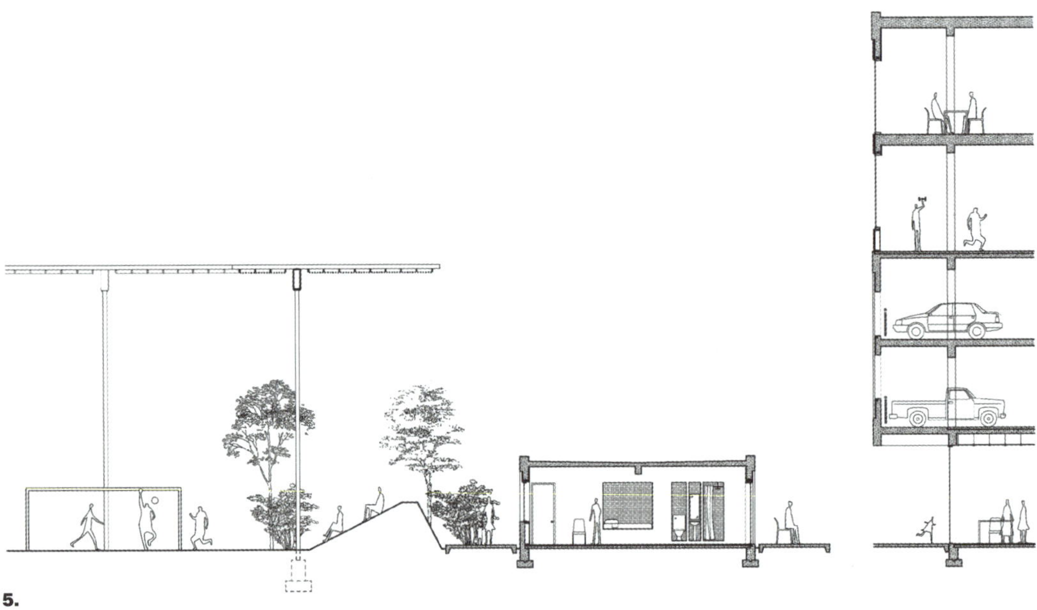

5.

6.

7.

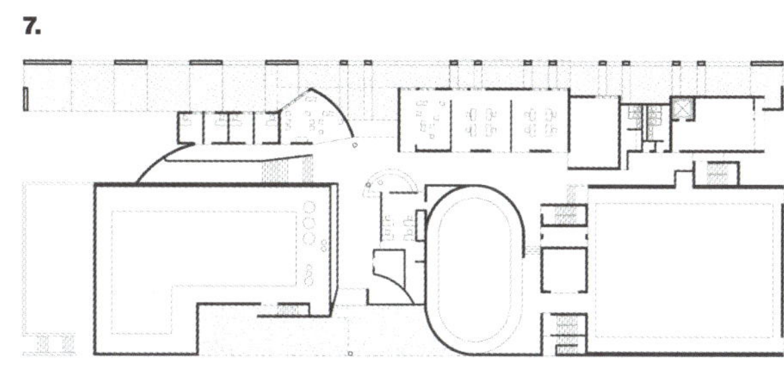

4. 1:50 Perspective
5. 1:50 Section
6. Ancestor drawing: YMCA 1:20 Perspective
7. Ancestor drawing: YMCA 1:200 Plan

GORDON SCHISSLER
COLLECTIVE MEGACHURCH

Ancestor:
Fire Station No. 4
(Columbus, Indiana)
Robert Venturi

The small church of the American village is in decline because of the effects of suburban sprawl. The people who once lived in the village are now living in these suburban areas, and have chosen the megachurch on the fringes of the big city over the village church. The Collective Megachurch, in North Canton, is a derivative of the megachurch that resurrects certain useful qualities of the failing small American church. Unlike the megachurch, which is composed of one large, generic arena, this proposal is a collection of smaller, individual churches gathered around shared public resources. For one thing, sharing resources alleviates burdens of cost. Moreover, this strategy preserves the specific denominations in North Canton while fostering a trend found in non-denominational houses of worship: an increasing acceptance of others. The project proposes a commons shared among small American churches as a middle ground around which the individual denominations can still retain a level of independence as they become increasingly lost in the homogeneity of suburbia.

1.

2.

1. 1:500 Perspective
2. 1:5000 Perspective
3. 1:5000 Site plan

3.

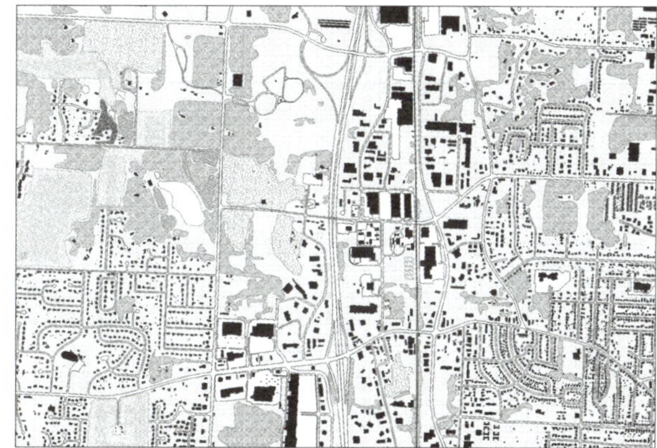

4.

4. 1:50 Perspective
5. 1:50 Detail section
6. Ancestor drawing: Fire Station No.4 1:200 Perspective
7. Ancestor drawing: Fire Station No.4 1:20 Section

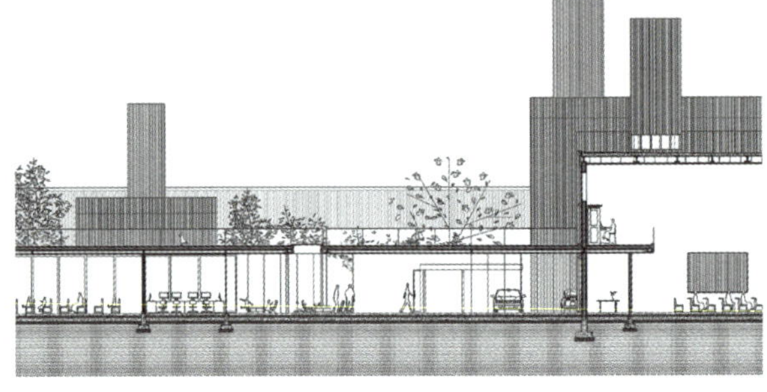

5.

6.

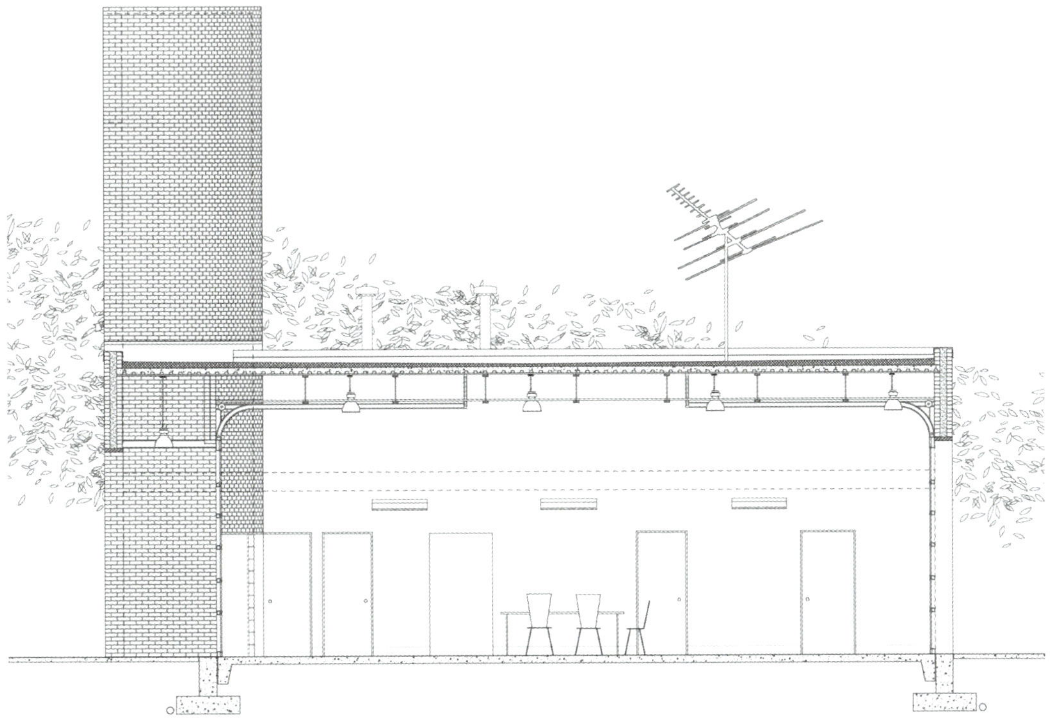

7.

JEREMY LEONARD
STARK COUNTY FOOD HUB

Ancestor:
Town Hall
(North Canton, Ohio)
Robert Venturi

Robert Venturi's unbuilt town center in North Canton, Ohio, would have been a drop of urbanity in an ocean of suburbia. The town lost its identity in the sprawl of its neighboring cities, Akron and Canton, and Venturi's city-hall program has been largely replaced by interactions on the internet.

A new commons for "the even covered field" is an aggregation and intensification of programs in an island, which is reached through a network of roads and train lines.

The Stark County Food Hub consolidates the county's farming and food distribution activities. Before the hub, food traveled an average of 1,500 miles from where it was grown, and more exotic foods traveled up to 2,500 miles, a problem exacerbated by the need to process the food prior to consumption. The hub is a big roof that covers a conglomeration of food production environments: year-round greenhouses, food-processing facilities, markets, restaurants, and food banks for regional distribution. The big roof is sized according to the land requirements that support the average American diet. Much like the thin façade of Venturi's city hall, the thin overspread roof is an image of this new commons.

1.

2.

1. Ancestor drawing: North Canton Town Hall 1:200 Perspective
2. 1:50 Perspective
3. 1:500 Plan

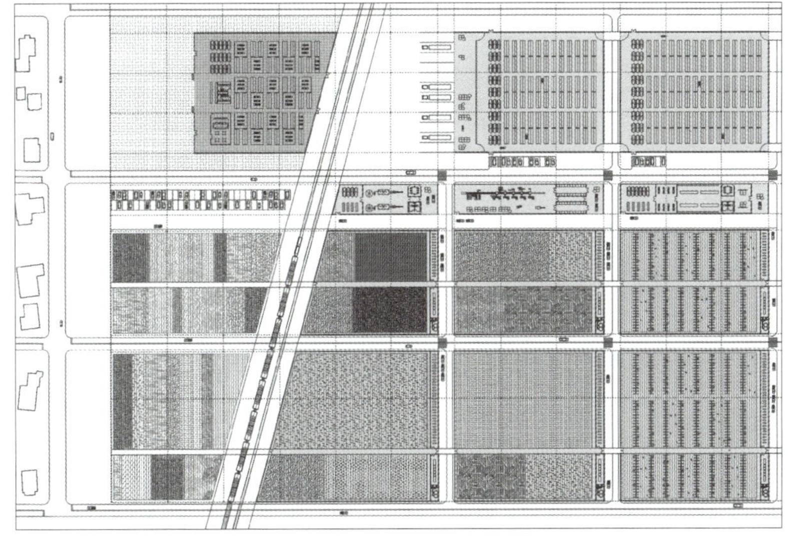

3.

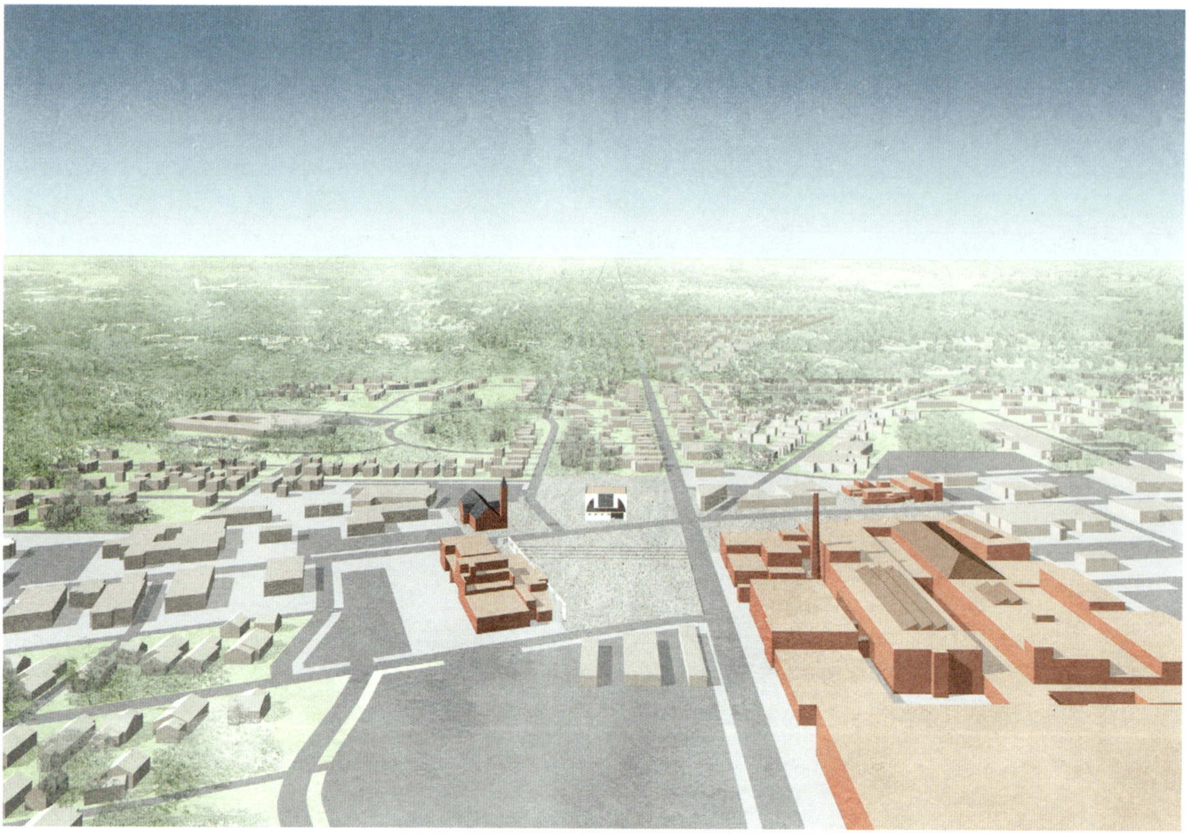

4.

4. Ancestor drawing: North Canton Town Hall 1:2000 Perspective
5. 1:50 Section
6. 1:5000 Perspective
7. Ancestor drawing: North Canton Town Hall 1:20 Perspective

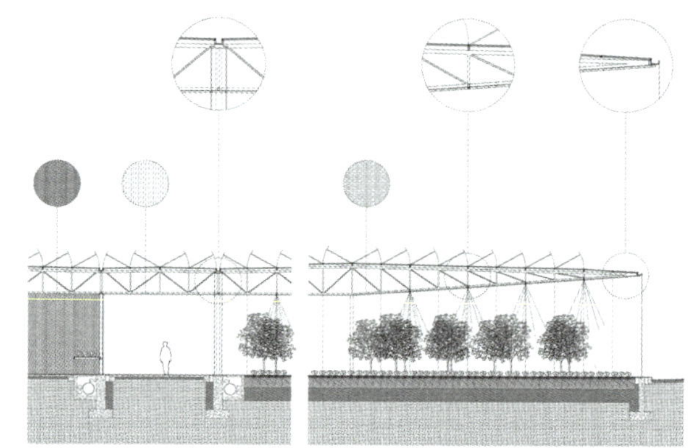

5.

6.

7.

KRISTIN NOTHWEHR
FARMERS' CO-OP

Ancestor:
United States Post Office
(Columbus, Indiana)
Kevin Roche

In the rural American landscape, urbanization has left a void. While profits in commodity crop production steadily grow, agricultural communities are suffering a demographic crisis in the form of an aging, male-dominated population. These agricultural communities increasingly face the problem of locating the scale of their shrinking communities alongside the large-scale machinery of their livelihoods.

This project will build a network of Farmers' Co-ops as a means of empowering owners of small farms through shared resources and collective bargaining. These structures, while economically driven, provide an opportunity to foster a commons that doesn't currently exist in the Columbus community.

The architectural proposal began with the landscape, which is experienced as a dynamic, horizontal line. This datum rises and falls according to the labor cycles of farmers, who experience periods of intense activity, followed by dormant seasons. The architecture responds to this movement, its own horizon set within the height variance of the crops, so that it is cyclically concealed and revealed by the fields around it.

The building's form draws from the Roman *horrea* type, an inward-facing, fortified, and centralized storage facility for grain or arms. Unlike the individually owned farm that grows and shrinks according to land acquisition, the co-op serves a finite quantity of land with a stable set of requirements for machinery, labor, and inputs. Thus, the project takes the form of a closed-loop system that defines a public interior.

A single entrance to this interior leads to a large courtyard space, the territory of machinery and logistics. Within this vast courtyard space there is the problem of dwelling. A second, nested courtyard within the larger perimeter houses the social commons, serving as a transitional respite between the home and the field.

1.

2.

3.

1. 1:50 Perspective
2. 1:500 Perspective
3. 1:5000 Perspective

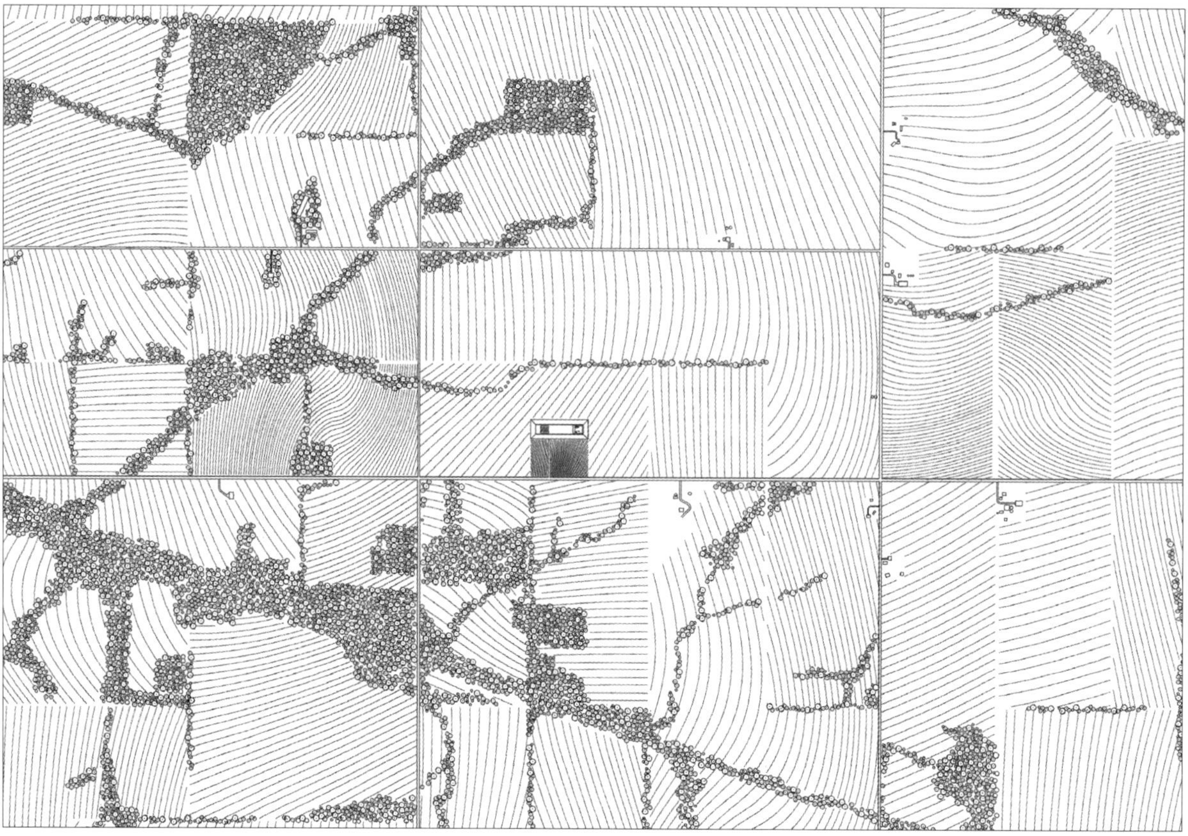

4.

4. 1:5000 Site plan
5. 1:50 Sections
6. Ancestor drawing: US Post Office 1:5000 Perspective
7. Ancestor drawing: US Post Office 1:50 Perspective

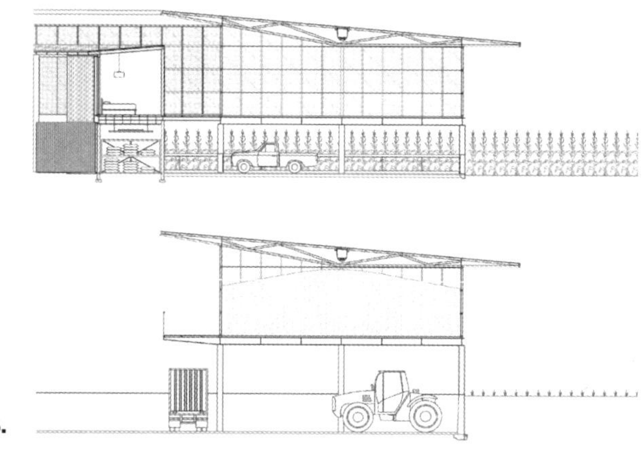

5.

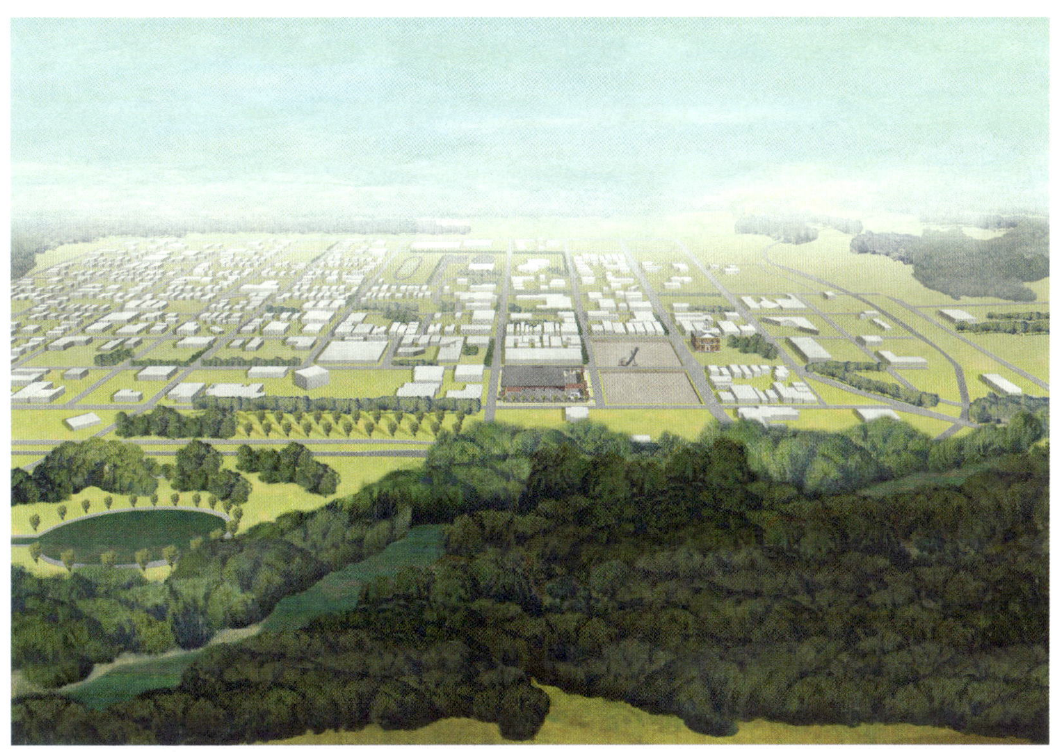

6.

7.

1.

1. 1:5000 Aerial perspective: compressed trees
2. 1:50 Section
3. 1:50

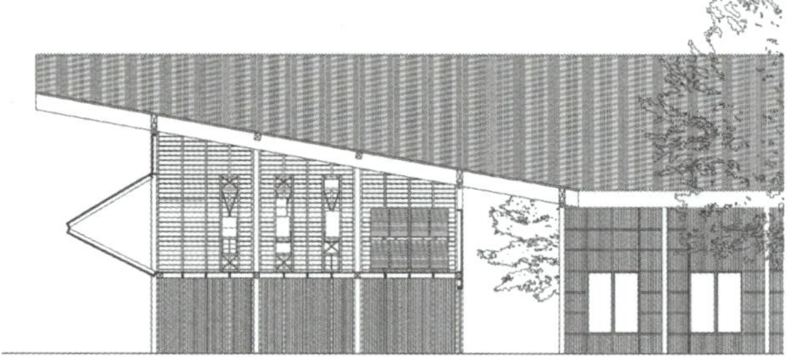

2.

MEGHAN LEWIS
AGRICULTURAL COMMONS

Ancestor:
Town Hall
(Borgoricco, Italy)
Aldo Rossi

Page County, Iowa, is dominated physically and economically by the industrial production of corn and soybeans. Eighty-eight percent of the land is for agricultural production, and only one percent is for residential use. The population of Page County and Clarinda, its largest town, is also a monoculture: 60 percent of Clarinda is male, and 93 percent is white. Dependence on industrial agriculture results in the dominance of machine labor, with the average farm in Page County holding over $200,000 of equipment.

There is a population crisis in agricultural counties across the U.S. that Page County exemplifies. The challenge of this proposal is to stimulate the agricultural monoculture of Iowa, making farming financially and culturally accessible to a new, younger population.

This project takes on the basic program of a co-op, including the machinery, storage, and silos, all of which operate at the scale of the township. Thus the co-op positions itself as the communal and commercial center of Coin, Iowa, and the surrounding area.

The co-op negotiates two scales: that of the agricultural machines, ever increasing in size, and that of the residents. The project mirrors this negotiation through its roof, which is lightweight but able to cover the project's large footprint, and through its two façades, which simultaneously face outward to the field and inward to the town.

3.

4.

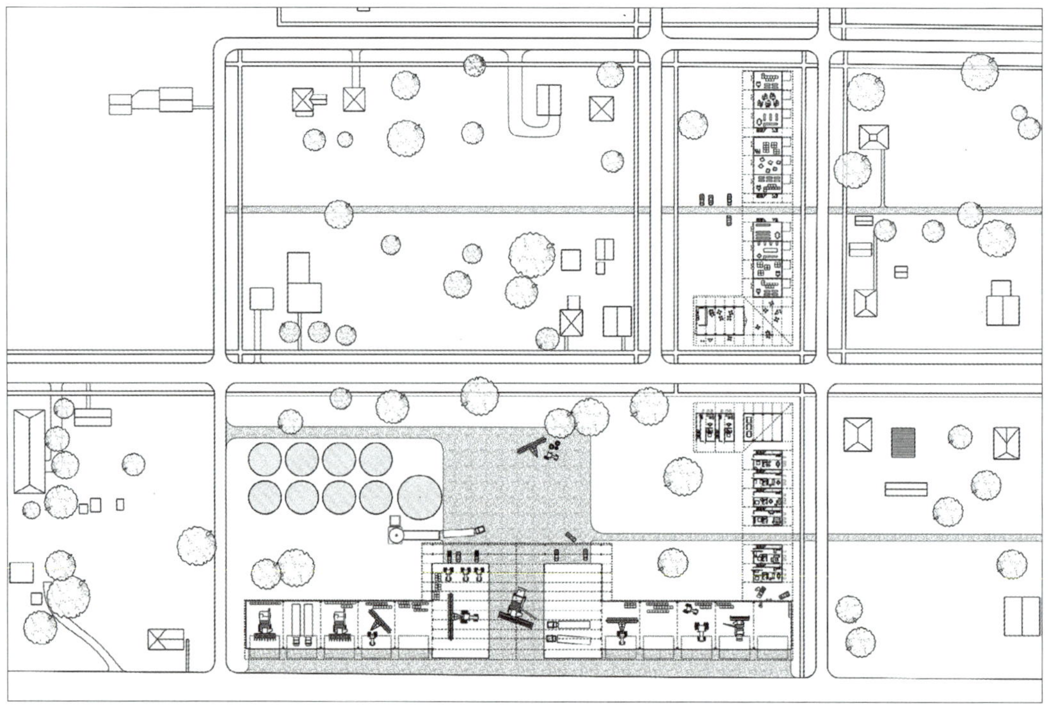

5.

6.

7.

4. Ancestor Drawing: Borgoricco Town Hall 1:2000 Perspective
5. 1:500 Plan
6. 1:5000 Site plan
7. 1:500 Perspective

SARAH KASPER
A CO-OP FOR FOOD AND FUEL

Ancestor:
Elementary School
(Fagnano Olona, Italy)
Aldo Rossi

While the shrinking population of farm towns across the United States has resulted in the atrophy of many normative types of commons, the farm co-op typology persists. With the growth of commodity farming, contemporary co-ops now serve the needs of a productive landscape that is focused on fuel instead of food. Reexamining the farm co-op typology, this project investigates the friction between these two types of productive landscapes, bringing them together in one co-op. This proposal also investigates the ways in which global fuel economies and local food production can work in tandem to redefine the rural landscapes of the American Midwest. This consolidation further represents a formal and functional shift in small-town governance, from that of the courthouse at the center to that of the co-op at the periphery. The expanded co-op typology centers around storage and the market, both locally and globally. Grain silos and cold storage for vegetables act as a perimeter for a large central hall that is open to both regional vegetable markets and global commodity trading. Grain elevators serve as a framework within which the commons of the co-op exists. At a more basic level, this new co-op acts as a visual marker on the flat landscape of Iowa: just as the courthouse once marked the civic center of the small town, so the co-op now marks the commons of a storage and market center scaled to the region.

1.

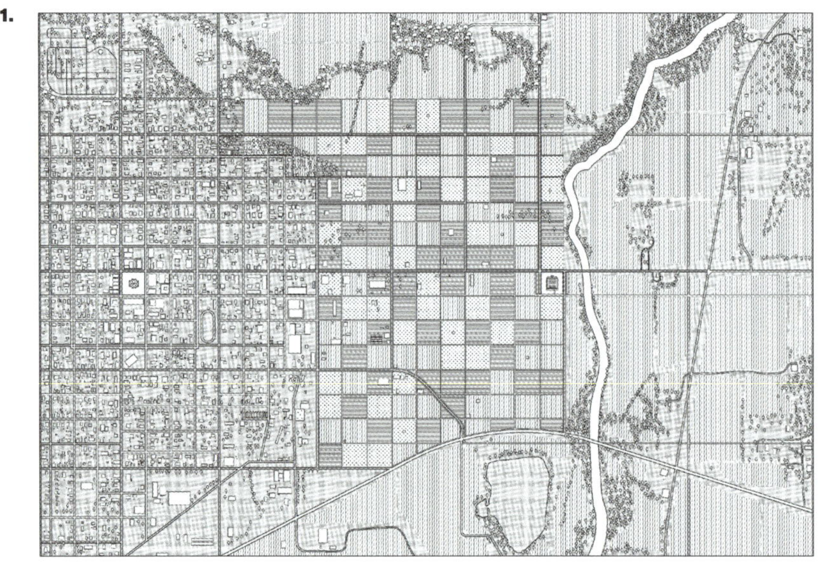

2.

1. 1:5000 Site plan
2. 1:50 Perspective
3. 1:50 Section

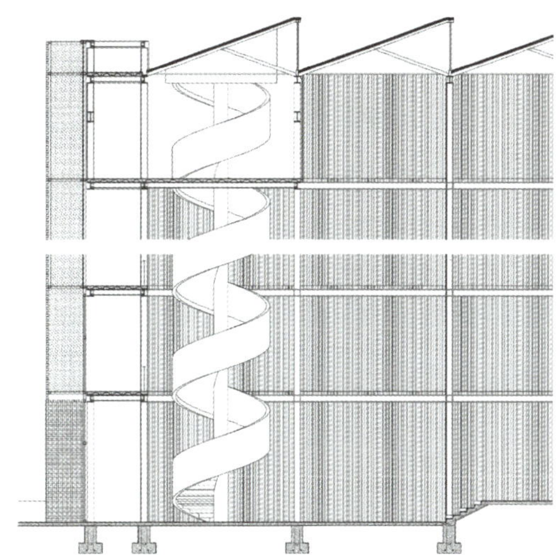

3.

4.

4. Ancestor Drawing: Elementary School
1:200 Perspective
5. Ancestor drawing: 1:200 Plan
6. 1:500 Perspective
7. Ancestor drawing: Elementary School
1:2000 Site plan

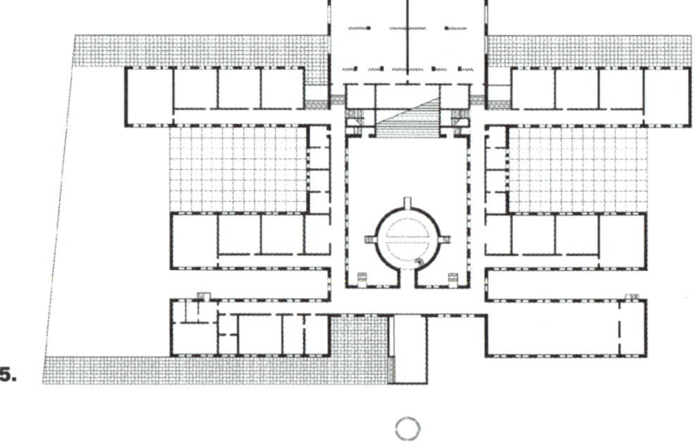

5.

6.

7.

SOFIA SINGER
THE AGRICULTURAL CO-OPERATIVE SCHOOL

Ancestor:
San Gaetano Thiene
(Padua, Italy)
Vincenzo Scamozzi

The most severe threat to the American village is the disappearance of regional rural knowledge from the village community. To anchor knowledge back in the village, this proposal suggests a new agricultural co-operative school, a repository and generator of collective, local rural knowledge in twenty-first-century America.

This project reinstitutes a rural center for agricultural learning by joining it to a network of co-operatives. The school sits, physically and metaphorically, between the residential grid of Clarinda, Iowa, and the vast expanse of fields beyond and liaises with the state of Iowa and takes advantage of its agricultural funds and programs, such as the Iowa Youth Institute Food Program and the National Farmers' Alliance's Youth Education Group. Students enrolled at Clarinda High School may take classes for credit at the agricultural co-operative school and learn the basics of small-scale farming.

Formalized agricultural knowledge is needed to replace the void in inherited knowledge. This project exploits the public school system, using its public role to serve the commons. Like a furrow in a field, the school marks a line in the ground between large-scale industry and small-town community, sowing the seeds for localized, collective agricultural production in the future.

1.

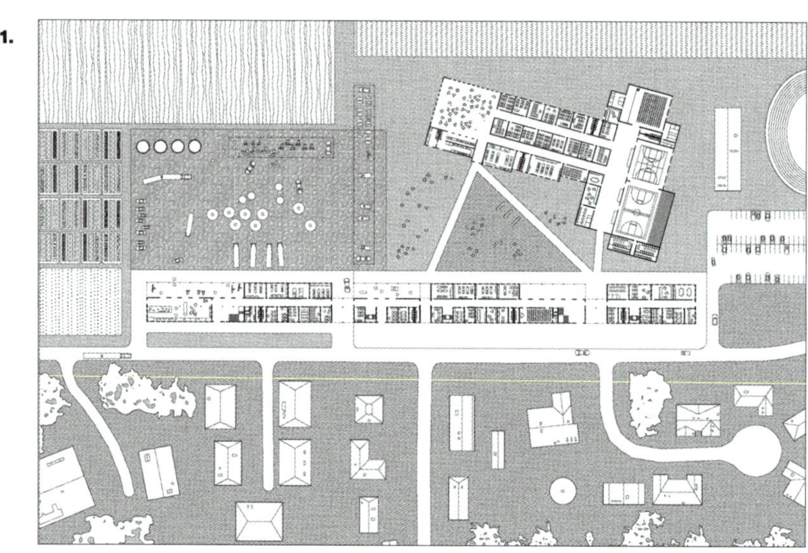

2.

1. 1:500 Plan
2. 1:50 Perspective
3. 1:5000 Perspective

3.

4.

5.

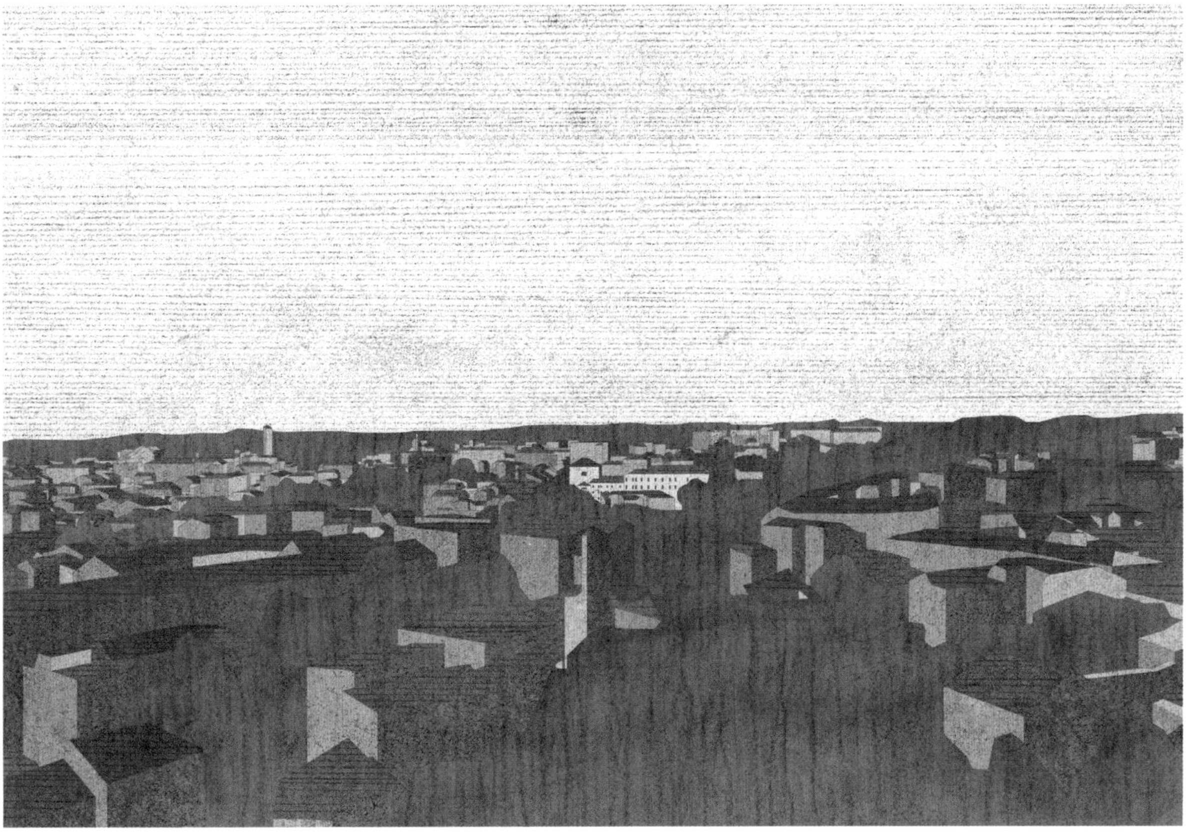

6.

4. Ancestor drawing: San Gaetano Thiene
1:20 Perspective
5. 1:500 Perspective
6. Ancestor drawing: San Gaetano Thiene
1:200 Perspective
7. Ancestor drawing: San Gaetano Thiene
1:200 Plan

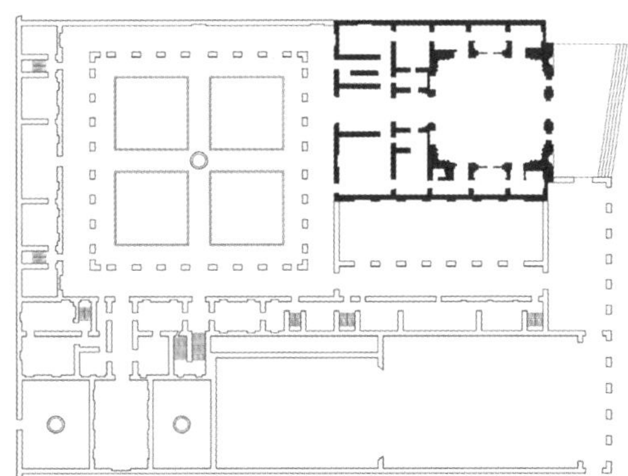

7.

JOHN KLEINSCHMIDT AGRICULTURAL CO-OP AND WATER TREATMENT FACILITY

Ancestor:
Procuratie Nuove
(Venice, Italy)
Vincenzo Scamozzi

Iowa's neat grid of roads and farms is broken by the crooked lines of streams and forests, making some of its land too wet or too steep to farm. Leftovers—unclaimed, unproductive, and unprofitable—are shared. Sited in that residual landscape, the proposed co-op engages industrial agriculture's role in creating another, darker commons: a hypoxic dead zone in the Gulf of Mexico where plant and animal life is choked by fertilizer runoff. The building itself is reduced to a single, relentless wall alongside a stream, with a simple roof sheltering equipment, grain storage, and offices. A series of low walls project into the stream, creating tiered basins that slow the flow of water to give wetland plants a chance to remove nitrogen and phosphorus. At each intersection between walls, small openings offer framed glimpses of this ignored residual landscape.

1.

2.

1. Ancestor drawing: 1:2000 Perspective
2. 1:5000 Perspective
3. Ancestor drawing: 1:2000 Plan

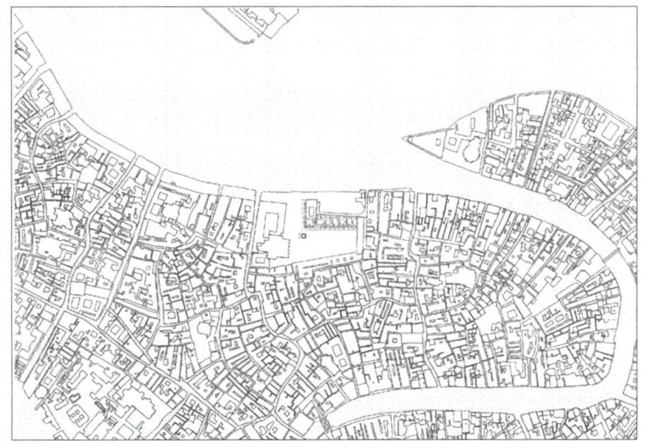

3.

4.

4. 1:50 Perspective
5. 1:5000 Plan

5.

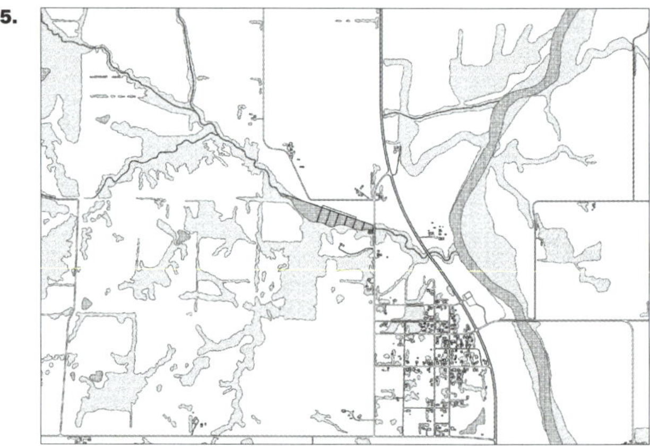

IMAGE CREDITS

OFFICE Kersten Geers David Van Severen: 3, 5, 6-7, 9, 11; Charles Anderson Kane: 18, 34 top, bottom, 35, 36 top, bottom, 37 top, bottom; Anthony Gagliardi: 18, 26, 27 top, bottom, 28 top, bottom, 29 top, bottom; Andrew Sternad: 22, 23 top, bottom, 24, 25 top, bottom; Carl Cornilsen: 30, 31 top, bottom, 32, 33; Gordon Schissler: 38, 39 top, bottom, 40 top, bottom, 41 top, bottom; Jeremy Leonard: 42, 43 top, bottom, 44 top, bottom, 45 top, bottom; Kristin Nothwehr: 46, 47 top, bottom, 48 top, bottom, 49 top, bottom; Meghan Lewis: 50 top, bottom, 51, 52 top, bottom, 53 top, bottom; Sarah Kasper: 54, 55 top, bottom, 56 top, bottom, 57 top, bottom; Sofia Singer: 58, 59 top, bottom, 60 top, bottom, 61 top, bottom; John Kleinschmidt: 62, 63 top, bottom, 64 top, bottom.

AESTHETICS OF

ACCELERATIONISM

ICELANDIC INFRASTRUCTURE, 2036–2056

MICHAEL YOUNG

YALE SCHOOL OF ARCHITECTURE

FUTURE REAL

THE LOUIS I. KAHN VISITING ASSISTANT PROFESSORSHIP

Contents

INTERVIEW MICHAEL YOUNG

NINA RAPPAPORT_How did you gravitate to the philosophers Graham Harman, Viktor Shklovsky, and Michael Fried and make their work relevant to your ideas on the aesthetics of architecture and realism?

MICHAEL YOUNG_It stems from a couple of things. First, it is an incredible responsibility we've been given as architects for what I like to call "the aesthetics of the background of reality." This requires a direct engagement with questions of aesthetics, specifically the aesthetics of realism. In terms of realism, one of the recurring debates in my aesthetics seminars is the misunderstood relation between abstraction and realism. We wanted to look at realism in a different light. Graham Harman argues for a philosophy of a speculative realism that focuses on the estrangement of the background and the ways in which one becomes attentive to qualities in the world. Harman argues for "aesthetics as first philosophy." Another person of interest to us is the Russian Formalist poet Viktor Shklovsky and his questions of defamiliarization, estrangement, and the ways in which one can problematize the steady flow of language in order to become attentive to it. Michael Fried is also interesting in terms of his writing on photography and on Courbet's realism. He was basically defamiliarizing French realism. He pointed out just exactly how abstract and strange realism was as an aesthetic.

NR_But realism was never about representing exactly what is there. For example, in painting or photography, the thing itself is already removed to the surface, and it becomes something different, something manipulated. Where do those philosophies intersect with your work? Is it about using your own realism, or is it more about how to teach an aesthetic theory in architecture schools?

MY_Aesthetics is more commonly talked about in art schools than in architecture schools, and this is something we'd like to change. Jacques Ranciere, who is interested in politics that are a result of aesthetics and not the other way around, sees aesthetic transformations as being what allows different communities and constituencies to come together and what gives rise to a political possibility. Ranciere's argument is that one of the major transformations in what is commonly labeled Modernism began with the aesthetics of realism in the nineteenth-century France of Courbet, Zola, and Flaubert, all of whom focused on details and descriptions of the everyday. Fredric Jameson's recent book *Antinomies of Realism* is about modern questions of affect rising at exactly the same time as realism. He notes that realism produced emotions that could not be named, thus it produced the experience of affective bodily states that didn't fit within the different kinds of Classical hierarchies of understanding those aesthetics. I think that is an interesting link because there has been so much talk about affect over the past twenty years. The discussion is usually related to novelty or exuberance, but the roots of affect can be found in a realism of the everyday.

NR_How can this be interpreted or used by architects?

MY_What we are trying to do in our practice at Young & Ayata is to make the background of reality important. For a design we did for a gallery show at SCI-Arc about the post-digital detail in architecture, we created a wall reveal, just like Fry Reglet's products, only ours did different things. If the normal reveal allows the white gypsum-board walls of modern interiors to float as if they never connected, our reveals tried to show just how abstract and decorative the resulting aesthetic produced by the wall reveal is. At its best, our wall-reveal interventions hope to not draw attention to themselves but to make the walls seem strange.

NR_The other concept you refer to is "representation." Your drawings and renderings are representations of buildings, but the representation is still something in itself. How do you work with that as a topic in your own work and teaching?

MY_Architects are always proposing alternate near futures that speculate about reality, so it is always a bit of science fiction, but more realism than fantasy. The questions of representation are fundamental to all propositions of architecture. So, we are trying to think about the status of rendering and drawing today, as well as materiality in relation to architecture, digital fabrication, photography,

Park View, Bauhaus Museum Dessau, 2015, Young & Ayata

and photorealism. Architecture is not a medium-specific discipline but, instead, one of multiple mediums.

NR_How do you teach representation in your classes at Princeton and Cooper? What have you taught at Yale before?

MY_Previously, at Yale, I taught some representation in the first semester of the second-year studio sequence. I tried to show that all aspects of architecture allow for the possibility, and plausibility, of it becoming real. The ways you handle the program and structure and organize the relationship to the site are different aspects of adjusting the architectural proposition. At Princeton and Cooper, I have taught different history and theory courses focused on representation. The primary issue has been how to understand the shifting paradigms developed over the history of architectural representation that open alternate conceptual problems through changes in the aesthetics of representation.

NR_Your object-making is part of the discourse on "the context as the building itself." So, how do you relate your buildings to their context? Is your aim to design a self-contained object rather than an integral element of its surroundings?

MY_Our discussion between context and stand-alone buildings goes back to Walter Benjamin, who said, "Architecture has always represented the prototype of a work of art the reception of which is consummated by a collectivity in a state of distraction." At first, I didn't want that, but I've come to

realize that the aesthetic power of realism is, by and large, not noticed. It operates subtly and allusively. How could the introduction of a new building begin to make the physical and cultural context it enters become strange?

NR_Some of your work appears to be autonomous objects, such as the Bauhaus Museum competition proposal for Dessau last year. But what you're describing is almost the opposite.

MY_A museum for the Bauhaus, in Dessau, comes with an enormous weight within the discipline of architecture. It was important to defamiliarize the dominant understandings of the Bauhaus associated with Walter Gropius and, instead, focus on the aesthetics produced within the Bauhaus workshops. The Bauhaus pedagogy was an aesthetic revolution that expored everything from textiles to theater, from graphic design to wall painting. The museum is to house the lineage of aesthetic experiments between craft, technology, and reproduction, which all came into a productive friction with each other at the Bauhaus. The work with color theory is one pedagogical example. The museum proposal is also sited in an urban park, not within typical urban property divisions. So, we proposed a cluster of singularly complete, repetitive figures – small, conjoined pavilions in a park. These vessels touch the ground only intermittently, allowing the park to flow continuously under the building. If you can insert a building into a site and make people see that site in a different way, defamiliarizing it and elongating their

Cône de Cadavre Exquis, 2016, Harmen Brethouwer with Young & Ayata

Plaza View, M.K. Čiurlionis Concert Centre, 2017, Young & Ayata

aesthetic involvement, they will think about their relationship to that place in a different manner. Ultimately, this is political. It creates the possibility of living in the world in a slightly different way than you thought of before.

NR_Why do you think art changes one's perspective better than architecture does – is it the immediacy or felt sense of freedom?

MY_Swedish architect Sigurd Lewerentz built some extremely weird things. He is typically discussed in architecture in a phenomenological vein, in terms of material tectonics and light. But if you look at his approach to typical, everyday details, there is an architecture engaged in the estrangement of realism. For example, in the church complex of St. Marks, he detached all of the rainwater leaders from the gutters so that the water has to jump from the gutter into the downspout, making you think about rainwater systems in ways you'd never thought of before. In another project, St. Petri in Klippan, windows set outside as a single sheet of glass are held with a couple of metal clips and glued with silicone to the outside of the brick. Viewed from the exterior, for a moment, all of the material is gone in the frameless reflections of the glass – it abstracts out. Then, from the inside, it looks like there is no window at all because there is no frame. It just looks like a big hole in the wall. That kind of architecture creates estrangement out of ordinary situations, yet it does not scream novelty.

NR_You don't talk about the visceral in your writings, but if you were to inhabit your renderings, they would be visceral. Are you interested in that aspect of aesthetics?

MY_We are interested in questions of sensation and affect and the way in which the body's senses can be triggered. We are not interested in the "truth" of materials but, rather, in the effects they produce. Can you do one thing and have its material effect be very different than you would expect? Some artists do this, such as Dutch artist Harmen Brethouwer, with whom we just collaborated on a piece. He only makes two shapes, cones and squares. The cones

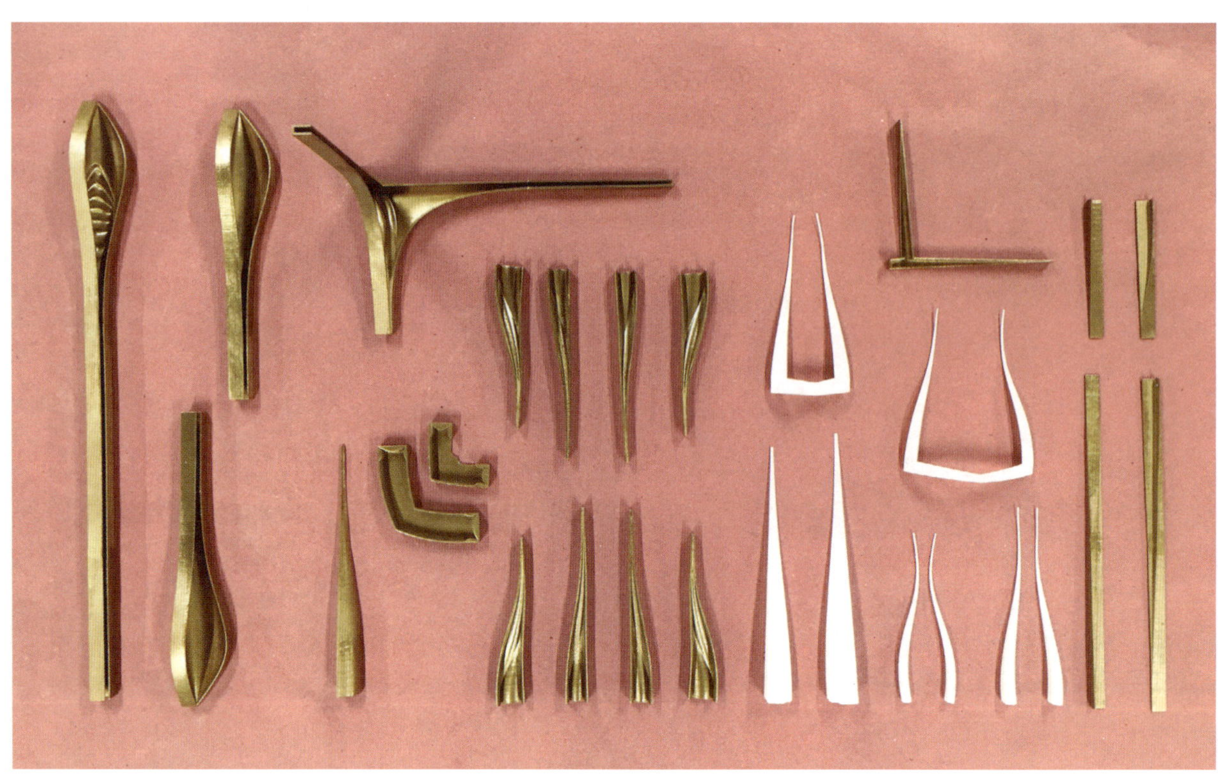

Reveal Catalogue, Wall Reveal, SCI-Arc Gallery exhibition, 2016, Young & Ayata

stand in for sculpture and the squares for painting, but he articulates them in every possible material technique and ornamental style throughout cultural history. This project produces a disconnect between form, craft, technique, and ornament. Traditionally, ornament and form are interconnected as an organic mastery of craft and material, but Brethouwer is creating a huge gap between all those things. It is a conceptual art project, but it is focused on ornament and craft. It makes you question what is real, what is artifice, and what is a technique or an expression. This is one of the things we are trying to do when we talk about the articulation of the building's ornament.

NR_How did you meet Kutan Ayata and start your office together? What led you to start a studio, rather than work on theoretical projects through teaching?

MY_Kutan and I went to Princeton together in the early 2000s. He currently teaches at Penn and Pratt. I've been teaching at Cooper and Princeton and at Yale on and off. We started the office in 2008. We shared enough similarities in design sensibility, but we also had complementary differences in our strengths and weaknesses. We believe in architectural design as a collaborative process, and the discussions that we have with each other continually challenge us to change and develop.

NR_What is the subject of your studio this semester as the Louis I. Kahn Visiting Assistant Professor?

MY_It will explore ideas of abstraction and realism in contemporary architecture. It will look at how architecture as a material artifact becomes influenced by, resistant to, critical of, complicit with, or progressively engaged with the aesthetic acceleration of contemporary crises. The students will look at the effect of this acceleration on the infrastructure of Iceland over a twenty-year period, from 2036 to 2056. Each student will be projecting a contemporary crisis into a built reality and documenting its development in the near future as if it were the recent past.

Corners A and B, Wall Reveal, SCI-Arc Gallery exhibition, 2016, Young & Ayata

STUDIO DESCRIPTION

THE ICELANDIC INFRASTRUCTURE: 2036–2056

"Don't start with the good old things but with the bad new ones."
Bertolt Brecht

One of the responsibilities the discipline of architecture holds is for the aesthetics of the background of reality. This is a loaded statement, so I will offer a few thoughts on each of the main words. With the term *background*, I intend something close to Walter Benjamin's observation: "Architecture has always represented the prototype of a work of art the reception of which is consummated by a collectivity in a state of distraction." As is quite often the case, the background of our environment is rarely the focus of our attention. But instead of this lack of attention signifying unimportance, it is exactly through this habituation that the background begins to have power, begins to establish the assumptions regarding the way in which reality appears. "Reality" is an even more problematic concept. In using this word, I do not intend to claim access to "the real." There is always something about reality that withdraws from us, something which we can never know or sense. In this way, aspects of what we assume to be reality are always constructed by personal and cultural imagination. This is more blatantly the case regarding the current situation of image mediation through our screens and devices. What I intend by evoking "reality" is more akin to an aesthetics of realism – not a copy of the real, but a tension between reality and its representation that disturbs or estranges assumptions regarding the way reality looks and feels. I also use the term to distance this statement from one of fantasy. It is a speculative realism that architecture is a participant in. The last word to unfold is "aesthetics." Aesthetics here refers to all the ways in which the world is made available to the senses. Distinct from the philosophical modes of ethics and epistemology, aesthetics relates to sensory qualities. It does not judge their truth or moral value, nor does it produce explicit knowledge about the way the world appears. Aesthetics may lead to the desire for knowledge or it may sponsor a change in behavior and ethical values, but it is not justified by these, nor is it the result of their claims.

One of the major environmental conditions classified as "background" are the objects and systems that are labeled as "infrastructure." These are everywhere, but they are typically ignored until they break. The things that we should identify are systems of distribution (roads, rails, bridges, tunnels, ports, aqueducts, sewers, cable networks, electricity, cell towers, satellites), production (petroleum, geothermal, hydroelectric, nuclear, mining operations, stock markets, factories), and storage (warehouses, sheds, distribution centers, data centers, parking lots). But this background infrastructure can be extended to other conditions that are often overlooked. For instance, nature can be considered as infrastructure, especially in the concepts of wasteland and wilderness. These are cultural constructions. The wilderness is usually considered as a protected zone where architecture is excluded or reserved to the most minimal intervention. The wasteland also excludes architecture, either due to the inability of humans to inhabit it or due to the toxic damage that humanity has wrought on the landscape. Even though these categories exclude traditional architectural development, they are often crisscrossed with infrastructure because we are continually looking for ways to exploit these sites. This exploitation could be extraction of resources, storage of damaged material, or even as an aesthetic commodity for tourism. The wasteland and the wilderness are examples of the creative destruction that capitalism unleashes as it always seeks to transform into new markets the raw background of our world.

In considering these expanded definitions of infrastructure, the island of Iceland becomes particularly interesting. It should be first noted that Iceland sits atop the rift between two major tectonic plates, the North American plate and the Eurasian plate. This geological location produces a large amount of geothermal activity on the island. Iceland also possesses a cold climate with a number of major glaciers. This combination of heat and frozen water leads to 99 percent of Iceland's energy being produced through the renewable resources of hydroelectric and geothermal energy. This abundance of

Section model by Heather Bizon

cheap energy has turned Iceland into an energy exporter. Two conspicuous manifestations of this are the metal-smelting and the data-center and server-farm industries. For example, it is cheaper to mine raw aluminum ore in Australia, ship it to Iceland to be smelted, and then ship it back to Australia than it is to process the material locally. The irony of the massive carbon footprint produced by shipping halfway across the planet to exploit renewable energy is obvious. The shipping industry itself is an infrastructural issue for Iceland. As Arctic ice recedes due to climate change, new shipping routes are opening, with Iceland quickly emerging as a hub of the industry; the fringe becomes the center. Iceland enjoys another resource, the natural wilderness. The majority of the island is uninhabited, largely due to the inability of many plant and animal species to exist in the harsh landscape. This wilderness has become attractive to three different types of inhabitants: the energy industry, the eco-tourist, and elves. These three have competing desires for the wilderness infrastructure, and their conflicts and negotiations are rapidly transforming notions of wilderness and wasteland. The interesting question is not which of these parties is more ontologically real, but how do these entities influence and alter the conceptual, material, and aesthetic development of the landscape.

Yale's fall 2016 advanced architectural design studio took the infrastructure of Iceland as a material and conceptual site

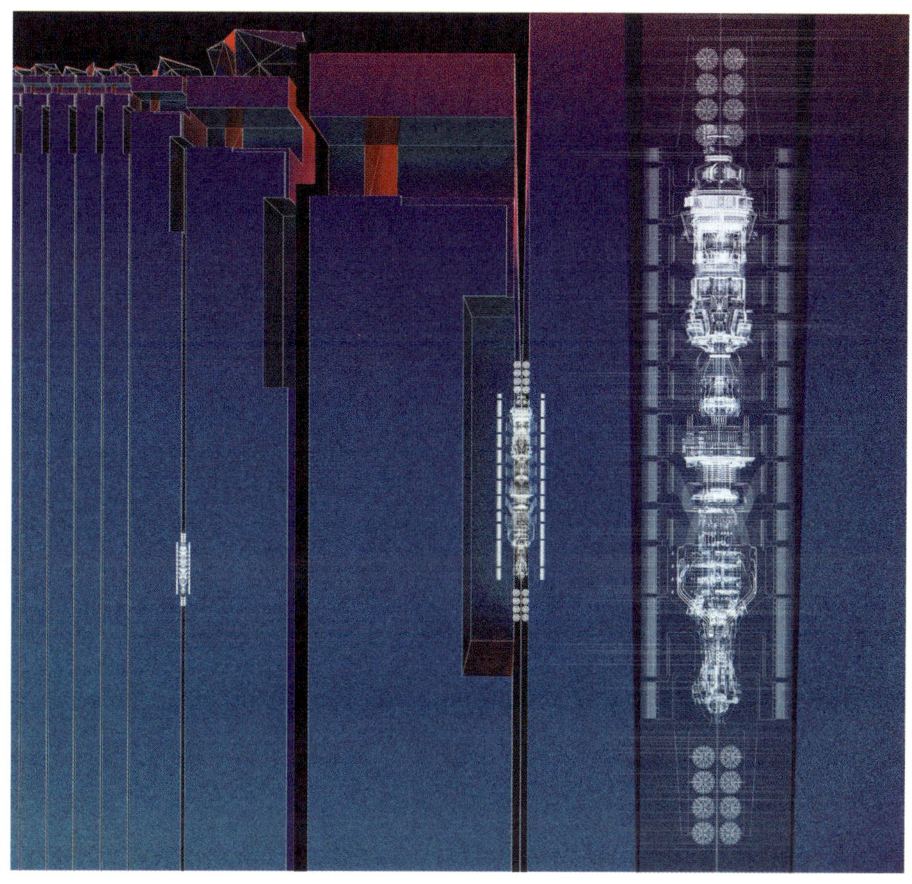

Section by Robert Yoos

to develop a series of projects. The studio brief had one crucial mandate: the students were asked to document the changing infrastructure over a twenty-year period, only this time period was to be 2036–2056. This assignment amounts to archival research twenty years in the past of a date forty years in the future. This temporal shift was important for the studio for three reasons. First, it was not a futurist, utopian-fantasy studio but an investigation into the near future, which we often call "the contemporary." Second, the shift from design proposal to documentary media is a shift in genre, not content. Finally, the move into the future required the students to play a role other than "student," disturbing the authorial assumptions that often stymie design speculation.

"The contemporary" as a concept describes the aspirations of much art and architectural production over the past half-century. We accept it as a real term to define what is different about "the now" as compared to a historical past or an unknowable future. But think about how strange and unstable the concept is once it is pried open a bit. First of all, when does "the contemporary" begin? It has to be longer than the ever-passing present, with its ephemerally fleeting transmission. We know this intuitively, because when something is defined as "contemporary," it is not that it is just present; it is always redefining the recent past and speculating on the near future. To say that an artwork or an architecture is "contemporary" implicitly locates it as important regarding the recent past and, simultaneously, that it will be important for a near future. This tension between near past and near future is a contradiction, impossible to ever experience and actually verify. "The contemporary" is thus a construct, a fiction, but one that we as a culture continually fabricate to help us make sense of what has just happened in relation to what we think will happen. An important aspect to note is that the contemporary rarely has the qualities of an escapist fantasy. Instead, it would be appropriate to describe it as a speculative realism.

Many discussions of the contemporary deal with the post-photographic nature of our current image culture. We are without doubt inundated with images in a way that no previous culture has been. This change is due to the proliferation of the screens that have become a crucial aspect of how we understand the world and to what could be called the background aesthetics of a photographic culture. The photograph has been an interesting problem for aesthetic theory throughout the twentieth century. At one level, the rise of the photograph marks the rise of an objective recording of the appearance of the world. Photography captures and indexes the trace of light on a photosensitive material, recording the objects that exist in front of the camera, regardless of whether these objects are naturally real or fictional constructions. This aspect of automatic and mechanical capture lends photography an air of epistemic truth toward the real, which was why it became such a valuable device for scientific objectivity. Yet, we all know enough to distrust the images that we see. Since the invention of photography, photographs have been heavily manipulated to produce fictions that appear to be real, and digital photography only accelerates this trend. Objects and events can now be created and put forward even if they never existed outside the space of the digital construction. Digital images are closer to abstract collages of discrete bits of luminous information than they are to any indexical trace of material existence. Yet, when we view them, we treat them as if they were photographs. The important distinction to make here is between a representational medium with its specific techniques and a genre of mediation with a specific structure of reception. Medium specificity is not very helpful regarding contemporary media arts. To expose the medium of a digital image does not bring a higher level of criticality, even if we enjoy the effects of glitches and low-res art. This disconnect is mostly due to the fact that the distinctions between abstraction and realism that animated so many debates throughout twentieth-century art discourse make little sense with digital images. A digital image is simultaneously abstract data and realist appearance. What matters more is to understand the genre upon which the image operates. A photograph can operate within the genre of the documentary, even if the content of the photograph is fake. In our current political climate, we are experiencing a crisis of sorts because all images have become suspicious. But, it should be said, all digital photography is post-truth; it is all a rendering of data toward an intended genre of reception. Digital photography engages aesthetic genres, not ethical or epistemological truth. This aspect is very close to contemporary architectural mediation in that, today, all architecture is designed through a digital interface. The digital model is simply a collection of data points that are associated in a specific manner to allow for a visual manifestation which the designer can evaluate. An architect must choose to render either an orthographic line drawing, an oblique projection, a physical 3-D print, a photo-real image, or a collage of disjunctive sources. These choices contemplate genre, audience, and intended interpretation. Because our digital mediations are all images formed through collages of discrete pixels and not the outcome of a process of dragging ink or graphite across a paper medium nor an index of light mechanically focused and chemically trapped on film, it becomes important for architects to understand how the intended genre operates so that the image engages. Each genre speaks within and challenges the boundaries of different conventions. For the fall 2016 advanced studio at Yale, the students were asked to engage the genres of the technical drawing, the satellite map, and the documentary photograph.

The agency of the author is one of the key questions explored throughout the second half of the twentieth century. These explorations include such notions as Roland Barthes' "death of the author" and Michel Foucault's author as part of an apparatus

Rendering from group work by Heather Bizon and Paul Lorenz

Rendering by Matthew Bohne

Rendering from group work by Matthew Bohne, Robert Yoos, and Aymar Marino-Maza

Rendering from group work by Pauline Caubel and Cathryn Garcia-Menocal

that functions to legitimate an artistic statement. For the purposes of the studio, there was an interesting displacement of the author function. This displacement took two different manifestations throughout the semester. The first half of the semester consisted of team scenario proposals, which required the students to take on the guise of a different interested party in the Icelandic infrastructure. These roles ranged from tourist boosterism and scientific research to private investigators and energy-company conglomerates. Each scenario was presented in the media genres appropriate for the roles the students assumed. Also, as said before, the studio is set forty years in the future, which creates another distancing mechanism for the work. In the second half of the semester, each of the students concentrated on individual work. The framework was shifted to a summit and exhibition on Icelandic infrastructure, between 2036-2056. The students became invited experts who had been hired to document specific aspects of the changing infrastructure. The design proposals were no longer considered to be in the genre of "architecture school design project" but, instead, were seen in the genre of documentary. The temporal, performance, and media genre displacements all worked in tandem to shift the background assumptions of how one should design a piece of architecture. This approach also shifted the status of the final review jury, which could no longer comfortably address the work from the role of "architecture school jury" but were forced to engage the roles assigned to them by the students. This approach may seem to be an extremely "fake" mode of design, but I would suggest that we, as architects, are always engaged in a version of such displaced role-playing. We have different audiences and represent our work accordingly. The only difference in this studio was that we attempted to accelerate these tendencies in order to see them more clearly and engage their full aesthetic potential.

The last term that I would like to address is "accelerationism." This has become a very fraught idea in recent years, as it has developed associations with fairly extreme versions of capitalism that seek to destabilize the governmental regulation of economic development. We shouldn't shy away from these associations, for they do fall under the banner of accelerationism, and to ignore them would be irresponsible. But what I would like to say is that, at its core, the idea of accelerating a current aspect of the world into speculative futures is not a new idea, and it is not tied in any fundamental way to the expressions that it takes under various political ideologies. It is amoral regarding ethical positions. This quality could be seen as a fault, but it is also part of its allure. Accelerationism can become nihilistic, it can become anti-humanist, it can become technophilic, it can become dark. But it also has a firm root in the attempt to engage the real as it appears, without utopian or dystopian fantasies or nostalgic leanings to an imaginary past. The sentiment is summed up in the quotation from Brecht that introduced the studio: "Don't start with the good old things but with the bad new ones." The stance of the studio regarding these themes was to focus on aesthetics. And this focus is key to understanding a left-leaning, progressive version of accelerationism. The studio constantly attempted to ask what the world would look like if a specific trend or crisis were to be extended into the near future. This way of framing the studio promoted a rough accelerationism, one in which problems were not solved, rarified, celebrated, or nullified; one in which aesthetic propositions could lead to political questions. Although each project had wonderful moments of invention, it was the final review discussion that explicated the approach of the studio. In the final review, the students and invited critics had a three-hour political discussion about infrastructure, culture, ecology, media, economics, and architecture. To provoke discourse through aesthetics was the most exciting moment of the semester. And for this I have to deeply thank the students for their courage to take this leap.

STUDIO BRIEF

As a contemporary movement in economics, politics, and philosophy, accelerationism has received more and more attention over the past decade from a growing number of supporters and detractors. There are several different strains of this movement, but at their core, they all hold that the way forward in a moment of crisis is not to resist, reject, or return to previous epochs but to move forward through the conditions at hand and intensify aspects of the current reality, accelerating into what may come next. This studio looked at architecture as the discipline responsible for the aesthetics of the background of reality, and, through this, it attempted to speculate on these aesthetics by accelerating several contemporary crises into the near future.

If accelerationism is left to operate only through economics, technology, and ecology, it quickly moves into utopian, dystopian, or nihilistic tendencies. To counter these tendencies, it is necessary for a cultural practice such as architecture to deeply investigate questions of aesthetics. If these critical questions are ignored, architecture may become merely a subaltern of capitalism. Although architecture is intimately entwined in these concerns, it should not be seen as the result of these forces but as a cultural project that contributes to a developing understanding of how these concerns affect our built reality. Projections into the future can often become mere fantasy escapism. But an aesthetics of a speculative realism can produce scenarios that directly comment on our own moment in time by advancing a particular crisis into the near future. These scenarios allow us to critically engage contemporary problems, posing the question, "What would it be like if X were true?"

In many ways, architecture is always a future speculation. This can be as simple as proposing a new lifestyle for a client's domestic environment or as grand as imagining a new city with new social relations. This aspect of architecture places great pressure on the representations that seek to create the plausibility of this new reality. If the aesthetics of a future reality can be articulated to a point where the familiar becomes strangely other, these speculations can gain political influence—they can build new audiences, new constituencies. How architects have made aesthetic arguments through different mediations is of crucial importance for the discipline of architecture, both in the past and in the future.

Description

The semester began with a series of representational experiments that looked at the conventions of contemporary architectural mediation. Specifically, the students considered the aerial map, the technical drawing, and the documentary photograph. The goal was to challenge these conventions to explore their aesthetic and communicative potentials. This first month also consisted of readings, lectures, and discussions regarding the studio topic. The key readings were Steven Shaviro's *No Speed Limit* (2015) and Bruno Latour's *Drawing Things Together* (1986). Also, the students spent a week in Iceland visiting geothermal and hydroelectric power plants, former NATO bases, and the Icelandic wilderness, among other sites. One night, the studio visited a 400-year-old Icelandic Turf House, where the students participated in the construction of a foundation for a new turf house.

The site for the studio was Iceland. The entire island was considered as a potential site for the development of future scenarios. Iceland presents a unique setting for the issues of accelerationism. As first impressions of the island may suggest that it is remote and isolated, Iceland is strangely at the center of many global issues, ranging from data centers and climate studies to genetic research and financial investment. The studio engaged a few primary questions: how will the aesthetics of the background reality in Iceland be altered in the next four decades? What will be the role of architecture in relation to the different crises that exist today if we pushed those scenarios into the near future?

Upon returning from the travel week, each student team chose an issue related to the built environment that is currently in crisis today. They documented the state and impact of these issues on Iceland in the year 2036, as viewed from the year 2056. The future is now past. All forms of media were available for these speculations. The studio put special emphasis on plausibility, as established through representation, and the aesthetics of estrangement in realism. Each group of students developed and presented a complete scenario of the future Iceland. The midterm review saw each group structure the discussion through different formats of presentation, which ranged from promotional pitch and stockholder meetings to scientific debates and investigative reports. The material was given through films, brochures, photography, internet sites, and archeological artifacts, as well as drawings and images. These scenarios set the stage for a re-imagined "site" that consisted of specific programmatic, cultural, technological, ecological, and economic issues. In the second half of the semester, each student worked individually, developing an infrastructural design that would respond to this new reality of the future. Each of the projects documented the "new" infrastructure – which, at this point, would have been completed twenty years in the past, in 2036 – through physical models, mappings, technical drawings, and documentary photography. The final review took the form of "The Icelandic Infrastructure Summit: 2056," where the students took on roles that were pertinent to the scenarios they had developed, presenting their documentations through PowerPoint presentations and exhibition-format drawings and models. This arrangement required the jury to take on a role other than as a guest architecture critic. What ensued was a lively political discussion triggered by aesthetic provocations.

References

Steven Shaviro, *No Speed Limit* (Mineapolis, MN: University of Minnesota Press, 2015)

Steven Shaviro, *Discognition* (London, U.K.: Repeater Books, 2015)

#ACCELERATE The Accelerationist Reader (Falmouth, U.K.: Urbanomic Media, 2014)

Benjamin Noys, *Malign Velocities* (Zero Books, 2015)

Boris Groys, *In the Flow* (London: Verso, 2016)

Quentin Meillassoux, *Science Fiction and Extro-Science Fiction* (Univocal, 2015)

Leo Marx, *The Machine in the Garden* (Oxford University Press, 1964)

Bruno Latour, "Visualization and Cognition: Drawing Things Together" in H. Kuklick (editor) *Knowledge and Society Studies in the Sociology of Culture Past and Present* (Jai Press, vol. 6, 1986), pp. 1-40

STUDIO WORK

AYMAR MARINO-MAZA
From BIM to Garage Bands: The Rise of Energy Hacking

At the turn of the last century, governments and corporations appeared to be shepherding entire societies through tools such as social media and search engines. Due primarily to the internet and its applications, private space was forcefully pushed into the public realm, and people were alarmed.

One of the more controversial and publicized examples of this subversive control occurred in Iceland. Within the past twenty years, everyone across the globe witnessed the advent of the Mat, the Icelandic invention that reimagined energy distribution. Due to its powerful electrical properties, this geologically modified nanostructure was employed to dispense energy across vast distances with minimal losses. An invisible force field, it was completely embedded into the natural geology of the ground below. Dispersed across geothermally active regions of the globe, the Mat led to a decentralization of energy extraction at the local level, drastically changing the way energy was distributed and employed.

Companies quickly responded with products, from electronics to clothing, that were able to harness this energy directly. Leading this venture was Matrix Corp., which patented the Matrix House, a BIM-generated, fully controlled two-part building system in which energy was harnessed through the floor and contained by the roof. Hailed the experimental green building of the decade, it worked as a

1. Sectional on-site documentation of one Matrix House, adapted for habitation in 2056 (completed by the research team)

2. Photographic documentation of the Matrix House's interiors in 2056 (taken by the research team)

3. An original 2036 technical drawing of the Matrix House, showing the way the machine harnesses energy from the Mat (provided by Matrix Corp.)

1.

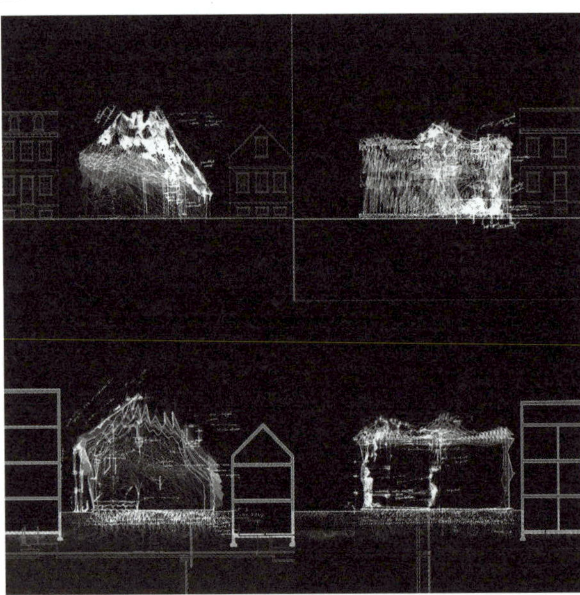

2.

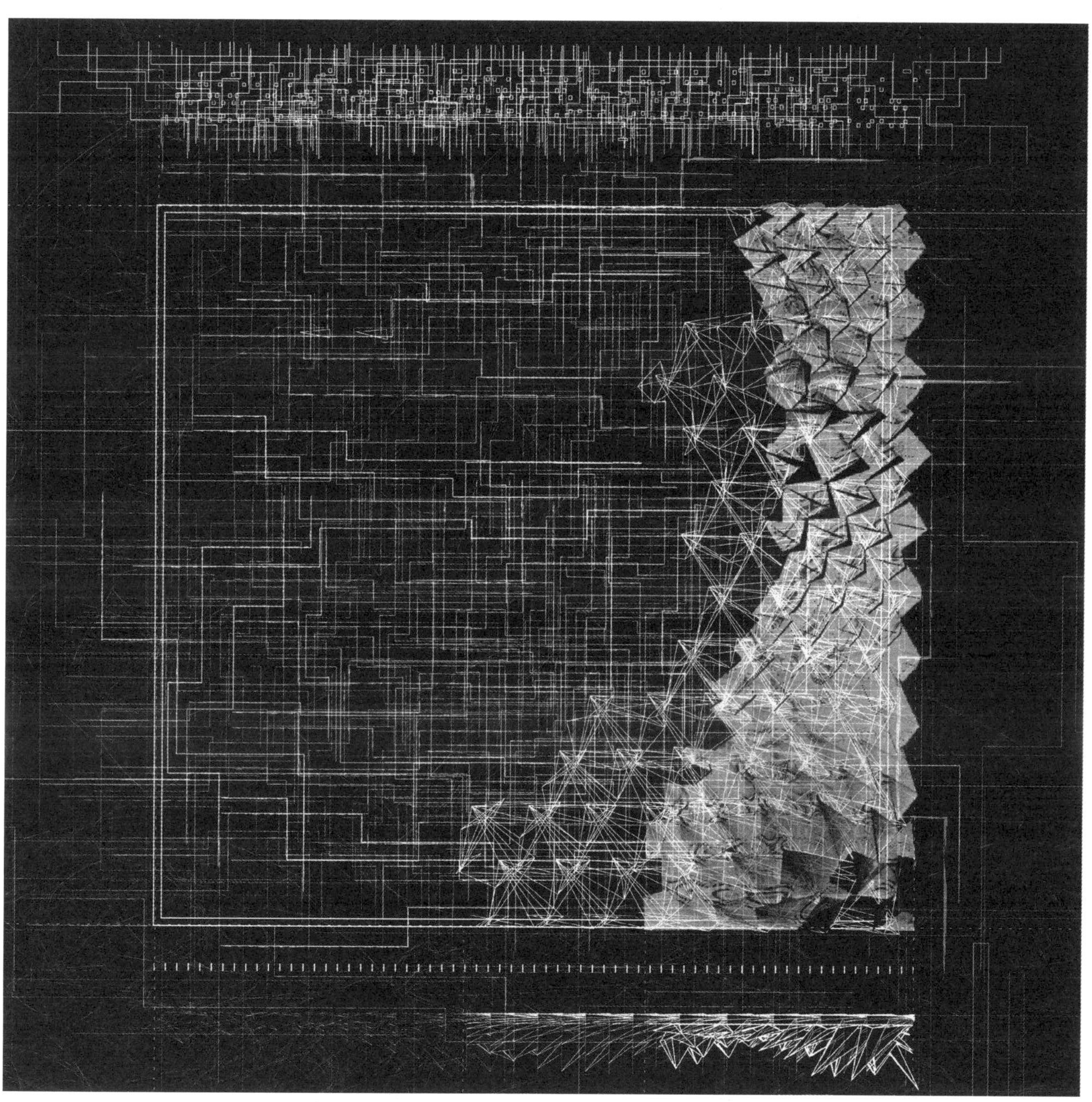

3.

sensor-equipped monitoring device that generated an interior that was adaptable and adapting to each inhabitant's particular needs.

Yet as these systems began to proliferate throughout our urban regions, the Mat and this new form of housing quickly faced worldwide criticism. These systems served to continually monitor and exploit its inhabitants for profit-driven intentions. These devices allowed the public realm into every home until the homes themselves became a form of control. Consequently, the project was abandoned, and many of the houses were vacated. Some of them still remain, left as remnants of the utopian dream of universal shared energy. But they have once again come under scrutiny because, though thought to be in disuse, new evidence proves otherwise. This documentation describes what has happened to these spaces and how they have given rise to the phenomenon of energy hacking.

4.

4. A scan of the electromagmatic energy of a Matrix House in use, 2056 (taken by the research team)

5. Photographic documentation of some Matrix Houses in Reykjavik, 2056 (taken by the research team)

6. Photographs of the original Matrix House, 2036 (provided by the residents)

7. Physical reproduction of a Matrix House adapted by residents in 2056

5.

6.

7.

CATHRYN GARCIA-MENOCAL

The Glacial Genome: Looking Back at the Mid-Atlantic Mediation Project

The pioneering Mid-Atlantic Mediation Project (MAMP) was one of the most important data infrastructure projects of the twenty-first century. Using a network of IASP self-boring probes, each fed by a fleet of unmanned air vehicles (UAVs), the glacier was translated into an ever-changing cloud of information and was therefore able to be surveyed and altered. The previously impervious megastructure of the glacier was converted into a responsive data set. Much in the way that galaxies, governments, and genomes are meticulously mapped, the MAMP produced incredible infrastructural architectures and an intimate understanding of our terrestrial home. Dr. Cathryn Garcia-Menocal has spent nearly two decades analyzing and altering the glacial terrain. Her work with the MAMP laboratory was critical to the Glacial Steerage Movement of 2032 and saved thousands of lives during the Great Seismic Waves of 2040.

1. The declassified exploded axonometric assembly drawing of the IASP-91 probe.

2. Archival photograph of a Sikorsky crane installing the probe in May 2036.

2.

3.

4.

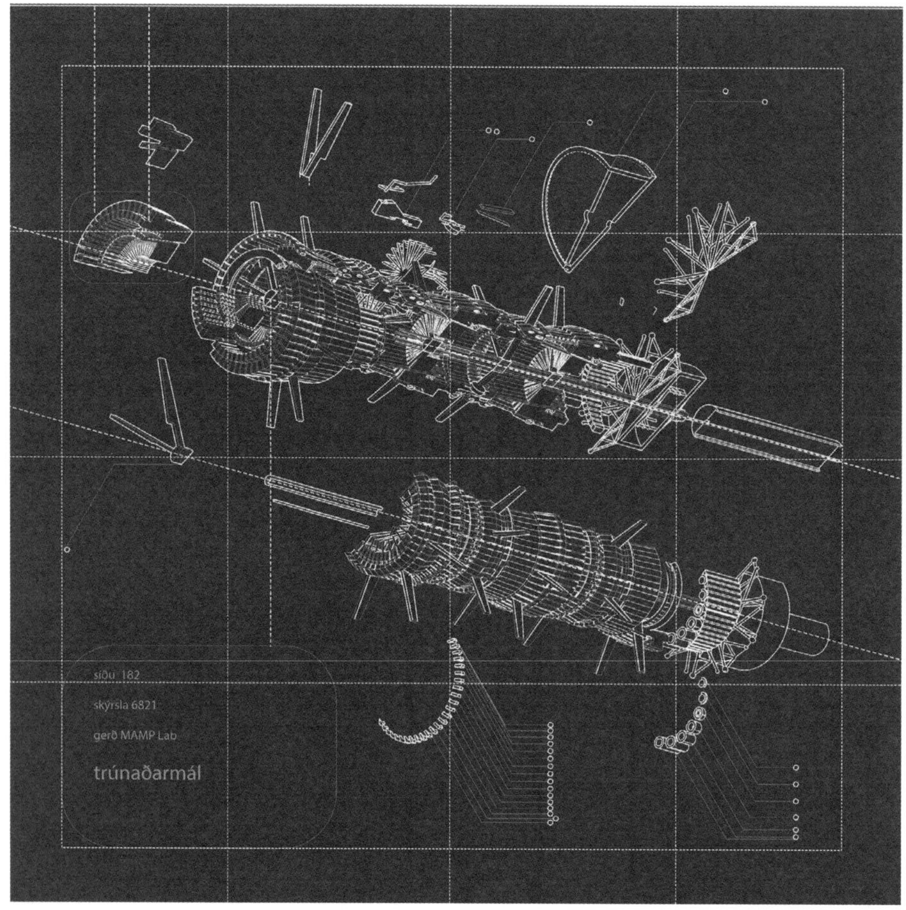

3. By 2056, the probes have completely overtaken the landscape.

4. View of the probe's exterior and its relationship to the glacier.

5. Plan of the probe: the tethering system, rotational cuff, drone chambers, and self-cleaning scuppers.

6. A sectional model displays the probe's mechanical systems.

5.

6.

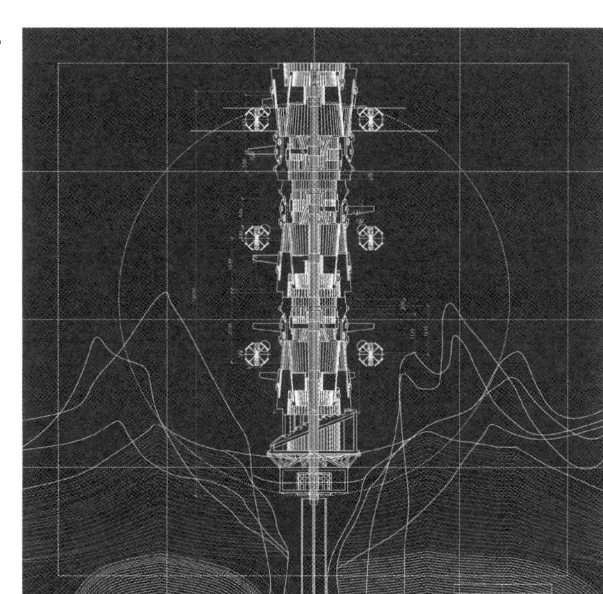

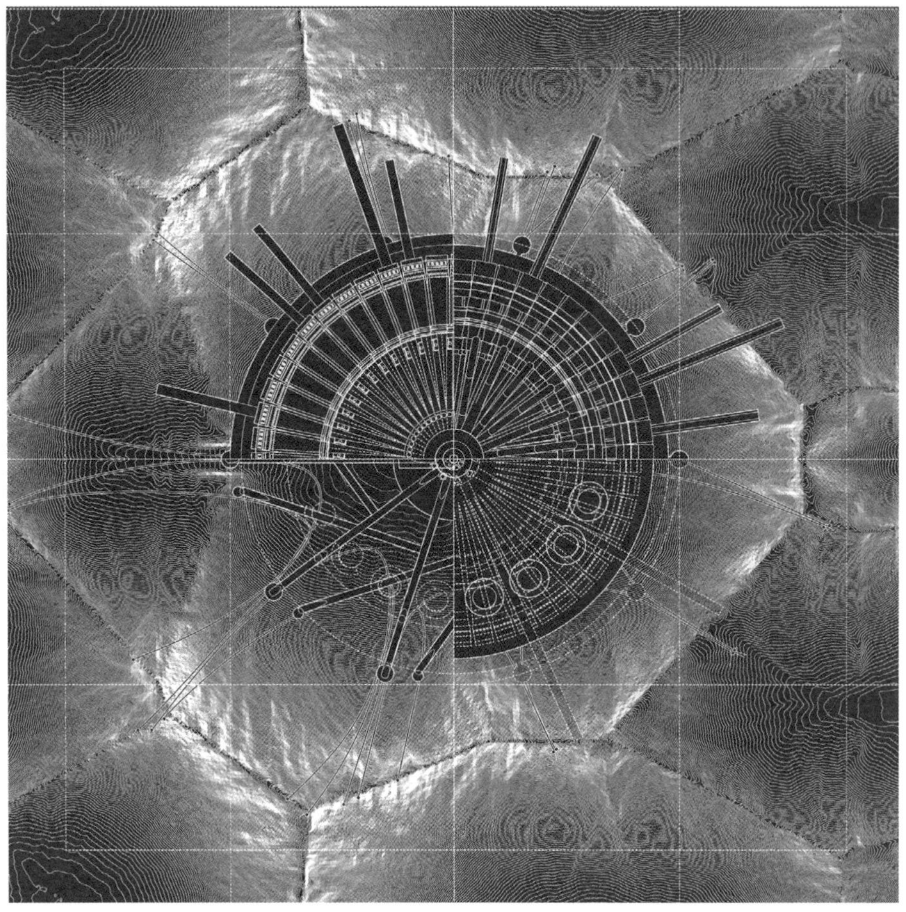

7.

8.

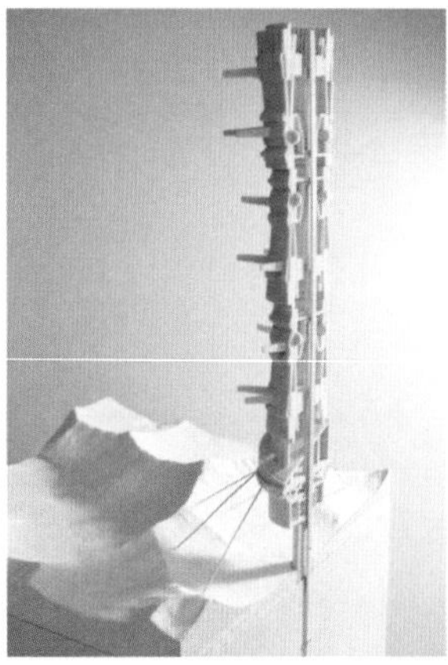

7. A sectional model of the probe shows the tethering system.

8. IASP-91 in its glacial context.

HEATHER BIZON
In Plain Sight

The vernacular is strangely timeless. Common to a place and time, it is foreign outside its context. What happens behind closed doors in the home has the luxury of remaining forever commonplace, as it is forever out of the public domain. Hidden within the domestic landscape is a public interface we have hitherto been unaware of.

In 2036, mysterious black boxes dotted Iceland's landscape. These structures disguised themselves as isolated villages. Seeming to be some of the most prosaic and banal structures in the modern Icelandic landscape, they were actually fragments of a global phenomenon. Off the grid from larger support systems, they worked in an extremely localized system, forming an infrastructure of isolated elements across the world.

1. We analyzed different scan conditions, cataloging the various typical and atypical distortions. This aerial drone scan highlights density of heat activity within the cluster.

2. What lies within the walls of these conglomerated houses is changing the landscape of Iceland.

1.

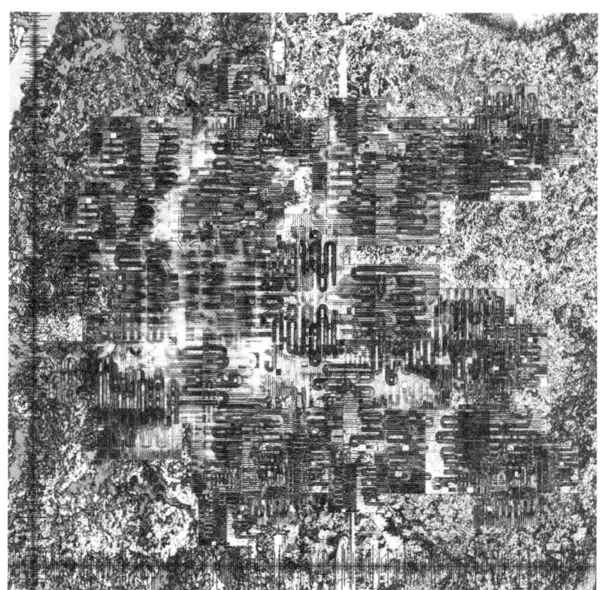

2.

In the late 2030s, the shed company Hexal began distributing prefabricated systems, positioning them in several locations throughout Iceland within proximity of these small, isolated towns. There is a massive interconnected network that is seen only at these nodes of consumption. This camouflaged infrastructure includes mines, power generators, processing plants, coders, hackers, satellites, undersea cables, transmission towers, and so on. Thanks to this concealment, what lies within the walls of the conglomerated houses has managed to remain timeless, even as the Icelandic landscape beyond has been drastically changing.

3. Imagery taken by local scientist to document the isolated but connected "villages."

4. At night, light is seen fluttering from the chimneys.

5. The light pollution generated by "villages" at 250 km (above local ground elevation) makes it impossible to accurately read the aerial imagery for further details.

3.

4.

5.

6.

6. Model Shot

7. Drone Footage

8. Very dense light conglomerations/clusters are evident in the light-density mapping of 2052, as seen by the satellite.

9. There are no signs of roads to or from the clusters. These localized conditions are often within 100 km to the small villages.

7.

8.

9.

MAGGIE TSANG
Data Landscaping: The Highland Dermis

Point your binoculars to the ridgeline of exposed rock at the edge of the Highlands National Park, where the tongue of the Skaftafellsjökull glacier spills out onto basalt flats, and you might glimpse the cresting pillars.

Barely visible from within Iceland's Wilderness Zones, this forest of slender server columns forms the neural surface of an extensive infrastructure of data harvesting and storage. In 2036, the Icelandic Tourist Board partnered with the Wilderness Management Agency to graft the barren highlands with massive computational capacity. Their plan was to develop the shadow zones beyond the tourist's LIDAR vision and free up new territory to support Iceland's symbiotic industries of tourism and conservation.

For almost two decades now, this hinterland back-of-house has been home to the nation's densest, and fastest-growing, collection of server columns. Here, the Earth's crust is made of rare metals. Cobalt, tungsten, and indium are the veins within Iceland's basalt substrata. This uniquely engineered mechanical interface does away with the obtrusive cell tower and the bulky data center; instead, it collapses the hardware of data and heat transfer into a single compact system that disperses signal and mechanical loads across thousands of small nodes that blanket delineated swathes of unseen land.

Though the Wilderness Management Agency does not provide precise accounts of exactly how much data is stored in this underground network, independent estimates indicate that upward of 600 zettabytes reside in this system, powered by a renewable supply of hydroelectric energy. Storage of this magnitude and tens of thousands of sensing nodes allow for the continual monitoring and real-time analysis of backcountry terrain, making the WMA's data landscape the largest warehouse of ecological information.

Iceland's wilderness finds its twin in a vast landscape undergirded by data infrastructure. This low-profile "crowd sensing" opens up new possibilities for the discrete integration of computational capacity into new territories. This case study examines the scalable application of the Highland Dermis, from the construction of a single sensing node to its transformation of Iceland's hinterland.

1. Distributed antenna system thermograph

2. Terrain management sectors

3. Photograph for Icelandic Tourist Board

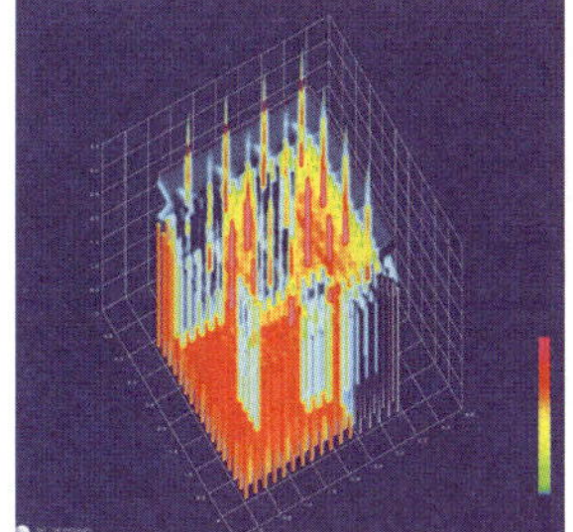

1.

2.

3.

4.

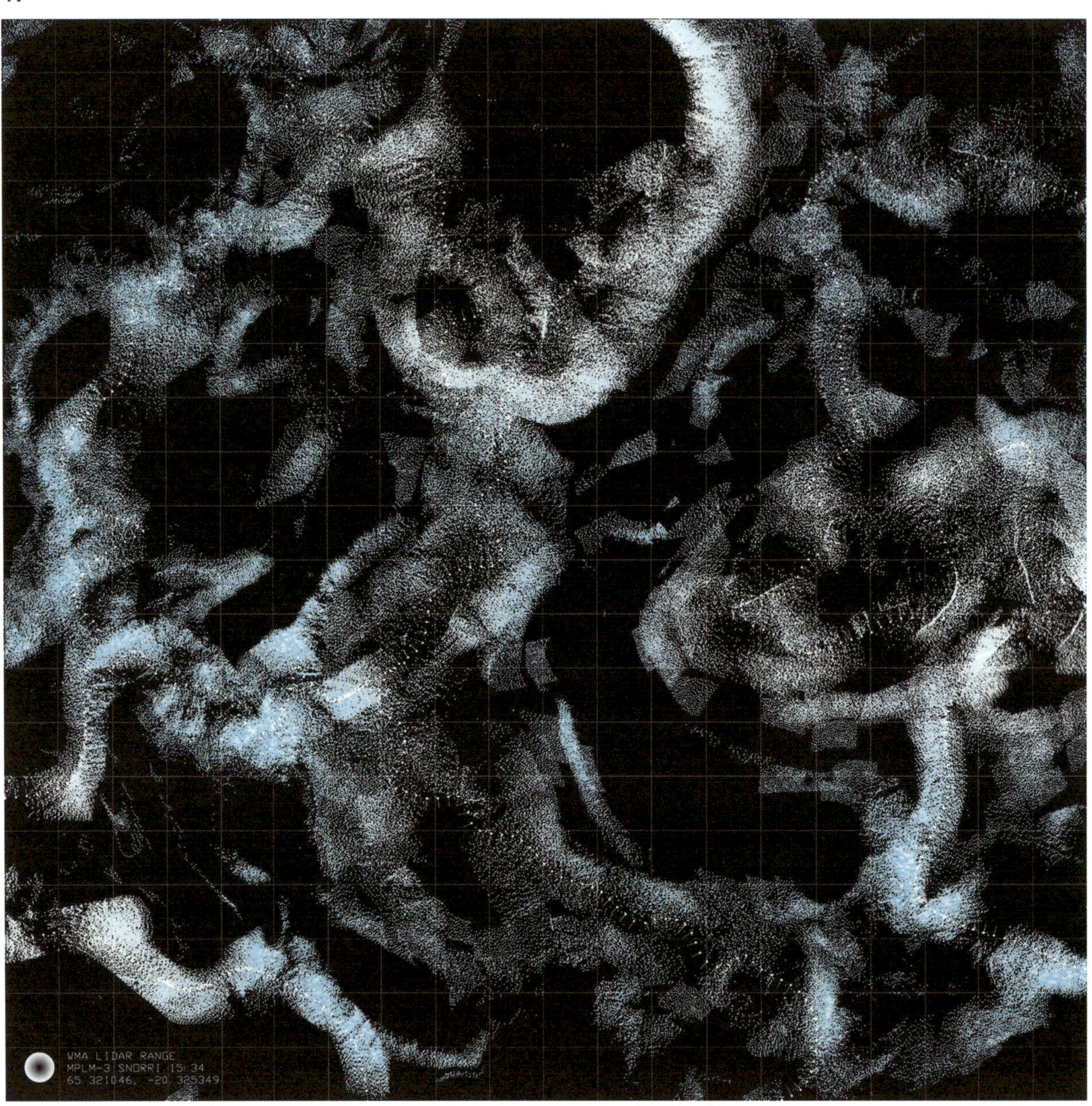

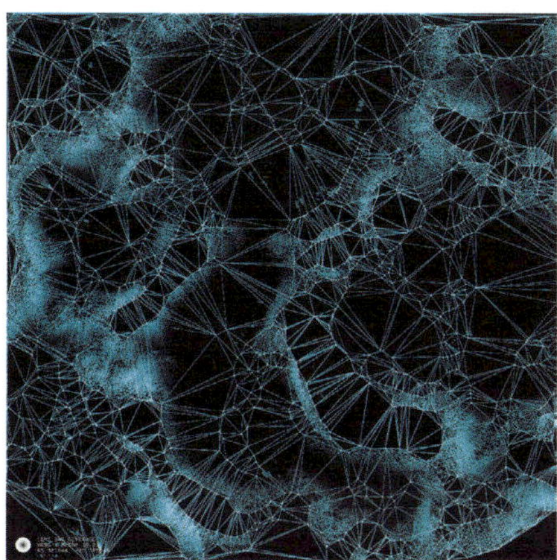

5.

6.

4. LIDAR trail map

5. Distributed antenna-system connectivity map

6. Visible coverage map

7. Distributed antenna interface detail

7.

8.

9.

8. Aerial scan

9. Terrain model

MATTHEW BOHNE
Iceland Resolution: The View from Nowhere

In Iceland, 99 percent of electricity is produced from renewable resources, 30 percent is from geothermal, and 69 percent is from hydroelectric production. In recent history, the demand for renewable energy has incited the increased use of experimental drilling and other energy-harnessing technologies.

Iceland is one of the most geologically active sites on the planet, providing vast and varied energy-rich substrata that make it ideal for geothermal drilling. Since 2020, Iceland has successfully developed two new types of energy production: the deep-drilling project, which taps into magma below the Earth's surface for a still-yet-undetermined supercritical point, and the joining of geothermal and hydroelectric power. Much of what we understand to be occurring below the surface of Iceland is still being developed, and there is only nascent research to speculate on the impact and long-term effects of these experimental projects.

1. Part of a subglacial structure that has ruptured.

1.

As commercial energy development accelerates, encounters with new dissolved solids, toxic metals, and corrosive gases increase. In order to meet the demand for energy production, Networx, a multinational power conglomerate, developed roving regulation and ventilation chambers that can be repositioned over ongoing mining operations.

The "beasts"–or dýrið, as locals refer to them–have become the sticking point in an argument between proponents of increasing the country's industrialization and those against it. The extensive drilling operation is hidden below the surface but marked by two-meter-wide surface nozzles. As the most visually dominant objects of the infrastructure are neither stationary nor permanently fixed to the terrain, a discussion of infrastructure's relative sovereignty has been provoked within contemporary conservationism.

2. At the microscopic level, the deposits have affected the composition of the terrain. By design, the roving chambers have left trails of sulfuric rock deposits, from the granular to the monolithic.

3. 1:50 Model

4. An inverted X-ray image shows the collection chamber and the equipment within – a peculiar relationship between phase change and synthetic structure.

2.

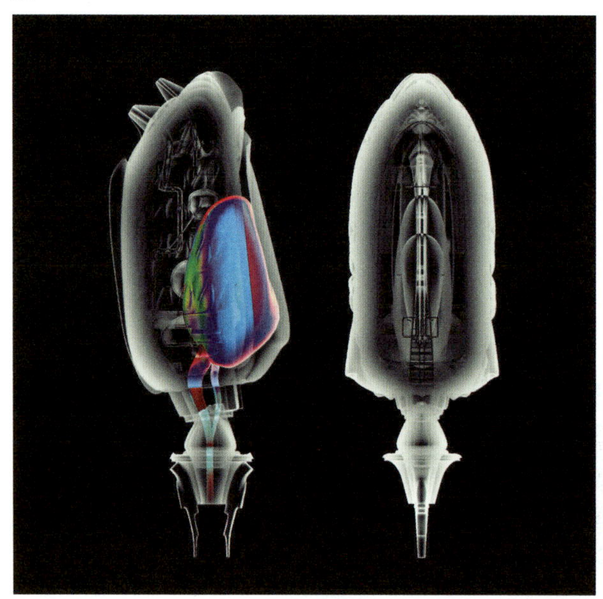

3.

23
24
25
26
27
28
29
30
31
32
33
34
35
36
37
Yellow and black sintered microcrystals
(typical nozzle development)
Yellow and black sintered microcrystals
(typical base development, abnormal terrain secretion)

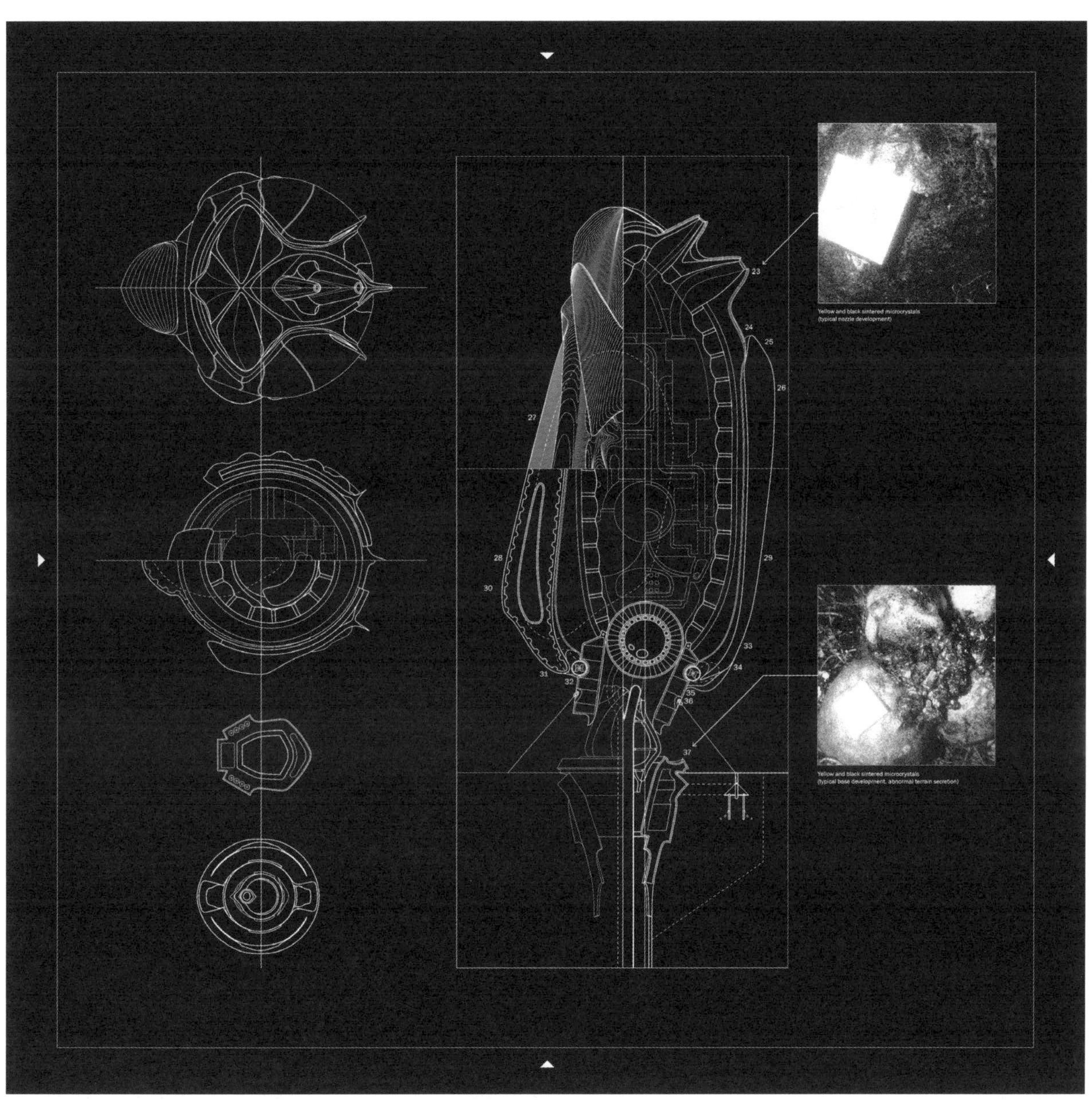

4.

5.

5. A small portion of Networx territories are mapped with a combination of vent trajectories and predicted outflow, with correlating heat maps.

6. Sulfuric and other metallurgic deposits are contributing to the now contentious Icelandic landscape.

7. The vents' flexible outer skin is continually inflated with sulfur hexafluoride, and an interior rigid structure protects the machinery.

6.

7.

PAUL LORENZ
Info State Infrastructure

The failure of the modern nation-state's internet policing power has had profound effects on both contemporary and historical patterns of state-to-state belligerence and especially state-to–non-state acts of violence. During last year's conference, Dr. Deborah Wood, professor of history and macro-scale computation at UC Berkeley, outlined her historical framework for understanding the rise of the trans-national Information States, tracing its conceptual origin to the post-Anonymous splinter groups. In Dr. Wood's framework, the twentieth-century obsession with class struggle is replaced by the twenty-first century's violent oscillation between supposedly corporeal and non-corporeal acting entities.

1. Chemical emulsion photograph, found in Reykjavik, of an inhabited pod interior.

2. Reconstructed infrared image of the field-study location

Dr. Wood used "Information State" as an umbrella term to describe the subculture of non-corporeal entities that operate in ways that negate aspects of reality that have served the physical body, including conveniences such as geo-located borders, material supply chains, physical militaries, and so on.

The non-corporeal entities that followed the 2017 fracturing of Anonymous maintained their disassociation with physical locality and retreated to virtual communities bound together by a shared small-group aesthetic.

The violent events of 2035 quickly crushed the illusion of powerless and ignorable Information States. We now know that the Second Siege of Sankt-Peterburg was enacted by the aggregated efforts of three of these non-geo-located Information States. While no direct violence occurred during the "siege," the effect of the digital encirclement was a simple re-enactment of 1941. The attack on the city's digital infrastructure propagated a complete collapse of Sankt-Peterburg's water, sanitation, electricity, transportation, and civil-response infrastructure. The supposedly non-corporeal violence of 2035's digital total war led to a catastrophic loss of life and marked the beginning of the robust hegemony of the modern Information State.

By extending Dr. Wood's framework, our team's ongoing investigation seeks to understand the relationship between the non-corporeal Information States and the corporeal physicality of the computation infrastructure they require. In tracing the digital activity of NCE33 (Nevyy Oktyabr), we have followed the group's obsession with the legendary Beowulf Cluster. Our research team, like the community as a whole, assumed that the Beowulf Cluster was simply a convenient name for any large, high-throughput slave botnet. Late in 2055, however, our network forensics collaborators in Charlottesville came to the shocking realization that Nevyy Oktyabr's concentrated decryption attacks, perpetrated between July 2049 and January 2050, originated from a single geo-located point.

At this year's conference, we will describe what we have discovered about the physical Beowulf Cluster site. While the hardware is six years into obsolescence, it may begin to explain the belligerent use of contemporary (possibly geo-located) computation clusters.

1.

2.

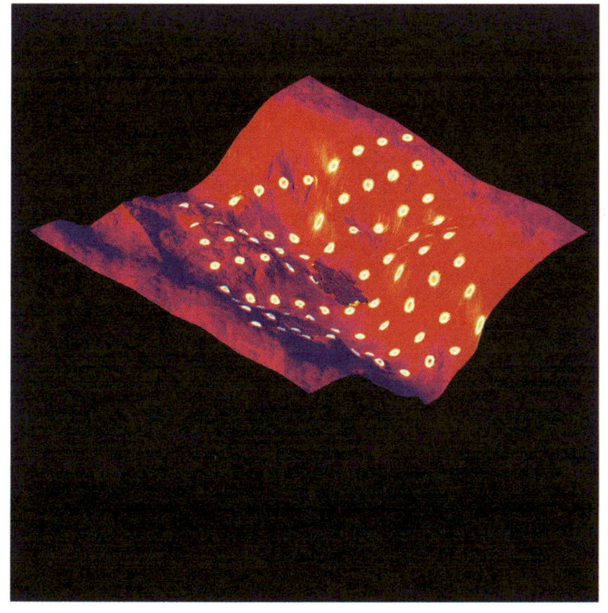

3.

4.

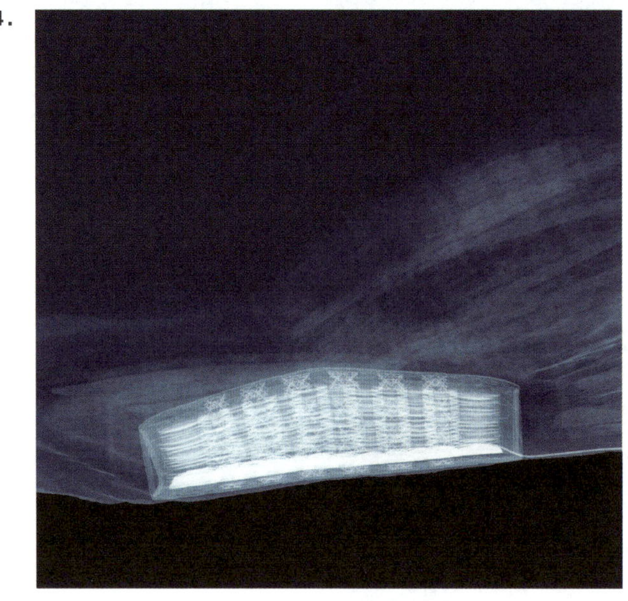

3-4. Reverse scatter x-ray images taken during 2036 field study

5. Chemical emulsion photograph, found in Reykjavik in 2036

5.

6.

7.

8.

6. Chemical emulsion photograph, found in Reykjavik in 2036

7. Digital photograph from last year's field study documents severe distortion of the pod surfaces.

8. Model reconstructed from field-study scans

PAULINE CAUBEL
Tesla Redoux: Iceland Probe System Report

Using the Earth as a conductor to transmit signals is not a new invention. In 2036, the Icelandic Probe System was first implemented in the most central glacier, Hofsjokyl. The probes proved to have a high success rate. The Icelandic glaciers became a site for wireless power transmission across the country. In recent years, this system has begun to be abused. As global warming has been accelerating, more and more of these probes have been installed across the ever-growing crevices across Iceland.

The prototype was developed by suspending mechanical-to-electrical energy converters inside naturally formed crevasses found on Hofsjokyl. Cables puncturing the glacier from all directions harvest the kinetic energy from the melting glacier. The friction and reverberations intensify as the probe's pistons are activated. The mechanical energy from the glacier is collected and transferred to the Tesla coils below. The energy then travels up the probe to transmit electricity between other probes. A system of stations planted across the crevasses facilitates wireless transmissions across Iceland.

1.

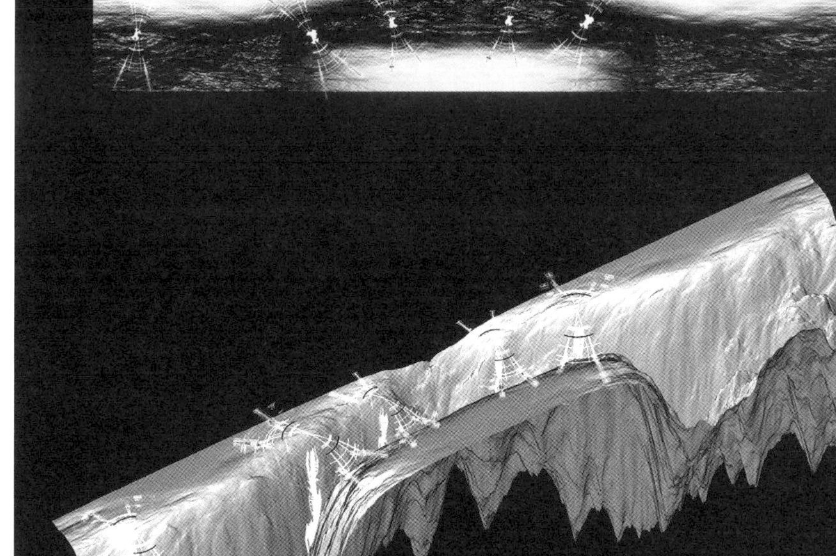

1. Diagram

Though these cracking glaciers revealed the escalating impacts of global warming, the Icelandic Probe System continued to exploit the economic by-product of this environmental problem. Soon, the increased amount of towers enabled transmissions to reach Europe and the Americas. What was once a sustainable infrastructural program has become a bystander in the exploitation of Iceland's landscape. And as the program grew in size, the cost of maintaining each individual probe decreased in economic value. As a result, probes were being built with less and less quality and shorter and shorter life spans. The defunct probes were not dismantled but left to disintegrate and collapse into the crevices.

The system's initial intention was to harvest Iceland's abundant energy sources with minimal intervention. But capitalist interests have led to irreverence toward the very landscape it was meant to protect. The delicate state of the towers and the environment it exploits is lost to the public.

2-3. Perspective

4. Sectional model

5. Aerial mapping of towers

2.

3.

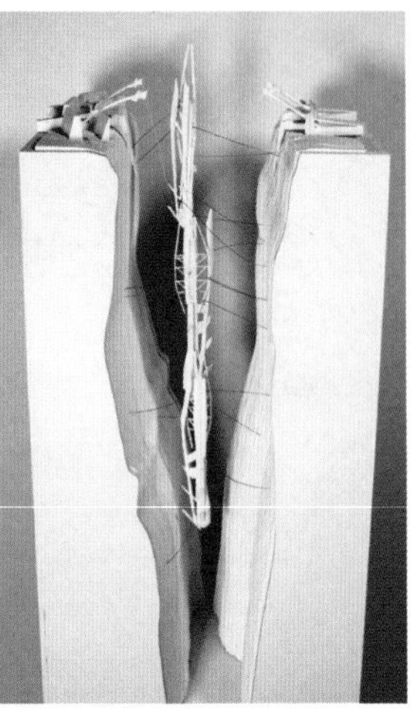

4.

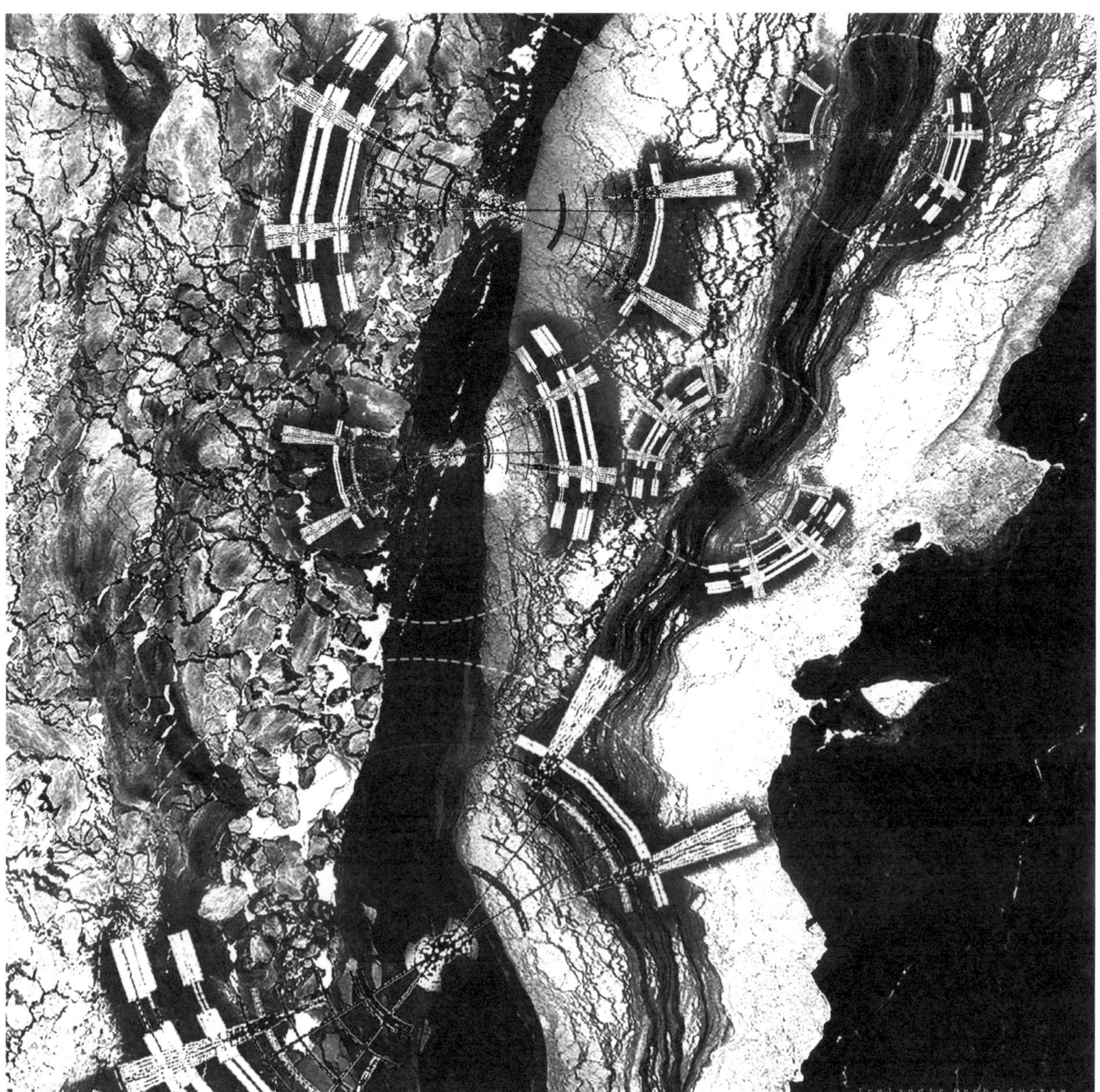

5.

6.

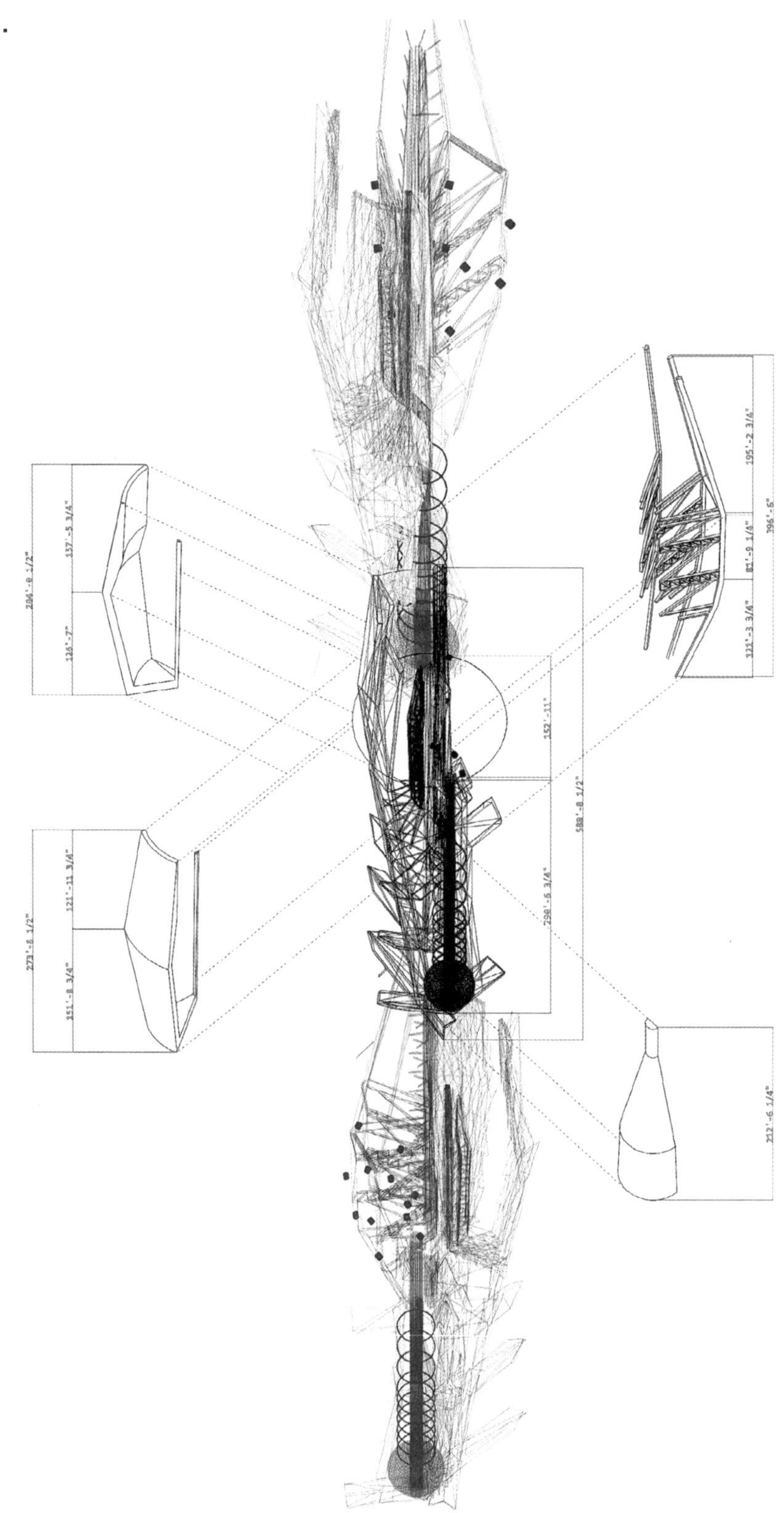

8.

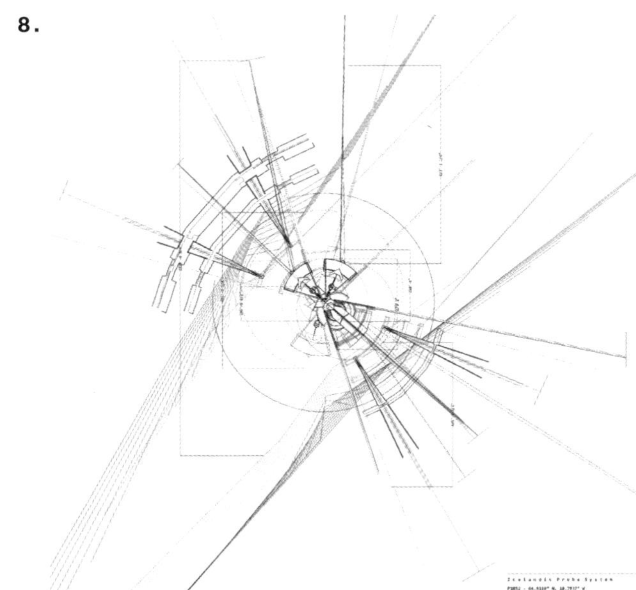

7.

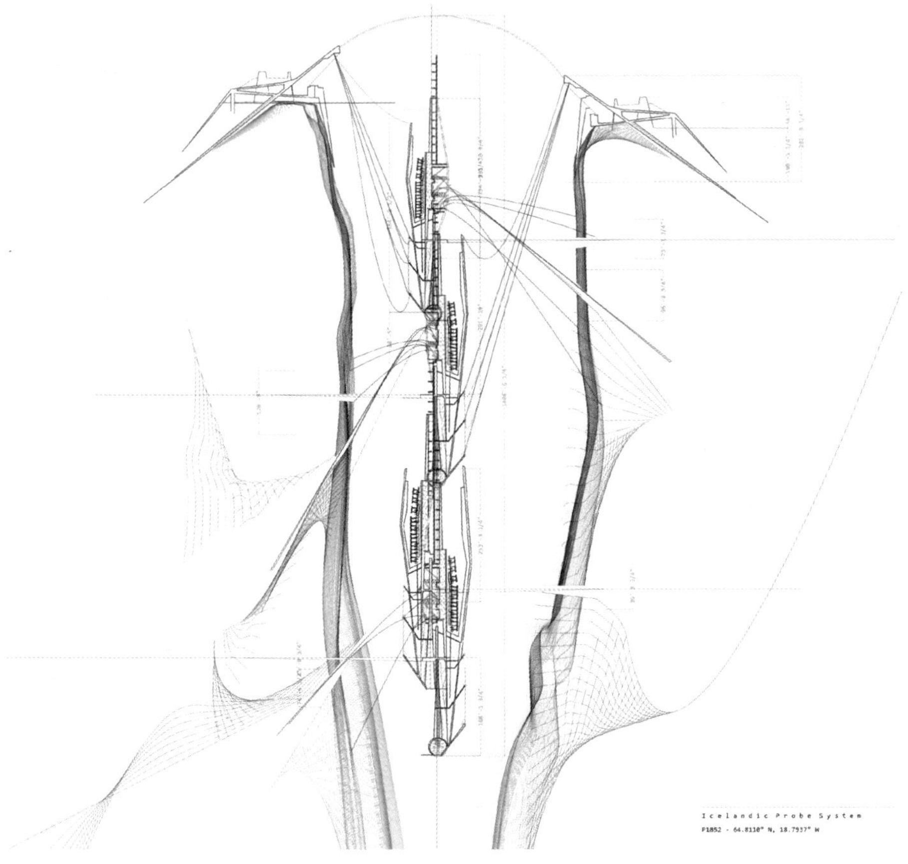

6. Exploded axonometric

7. Section

8. Planimetric drawing

ROBERT YOOS
Razor Mining: Refueling the Cloud

In summer 2020, experimental geothermal drilling operations conducted by the energy giant Networx Corporation yielded the discovery of a rare ore: phreatomagmite. Across the globe, the tech boom, coupled with the ballooning middle-class population, ravaged indium ore deposits for use in the production of LED surfaces and internet transmitters. The Royal Society of Chemistry predicted Indium's exhaustion within the century, which became a reality in 2022, leaving phreatomagmite as the only known replacement for the metal contained within all indium-dependent technologies. This dependence on phreatomagmite created a demand for new extraction methods to harvest this scarce ore that exists at extreme depths below the Earth's crust.

In 2024, the Icelandic government commissioned the Icelandic Mining Technology Initiative to develop a system for extracting phreatomagmite. The committee called for an economical mining operation that could sustain high pressures and temperatures while handling waste in a manner that would not drastically disrupt the appearance of the landscape. Terrabilden Technologie, a German mining and metallurgical conglomerate, was selected to lead the implementation of the world's first "razor-mining operation." Fully operational since 2036, the system has become increasingly embroiled in controversy over mounting ecological concerns. The terra-formed by-product has tested positive for the presence of extremophile organisms, believed to inhabit the deepest points of extraction. Many advocacy groups warn that this "drudging up" of scarcely studied organisms can have lasting, unforeseen impacts on the global ecosystem. Additionally, despite efforts to conceal the visibility of the access-road structure through algorithmically sculpted by-product, a growing number of government officials, scientists, and environmental activists have taken to the structure itself to stage protests against further continuation of the operation. Many tech companies and government officials, however, continue to advocate in favor of the extraction practices for the sake of the global internet economy and the general advancement of technology. The future of the project remains uncertain as the geopolitical implications grow increasingly contentious with each additional scar on the land.

1. Satellite scan of subterranean mining infrastructure, 2040

2. Drone's-eye view of razor mine, 2056

3. Main promenade with terraform overgrowth, 2051

1.

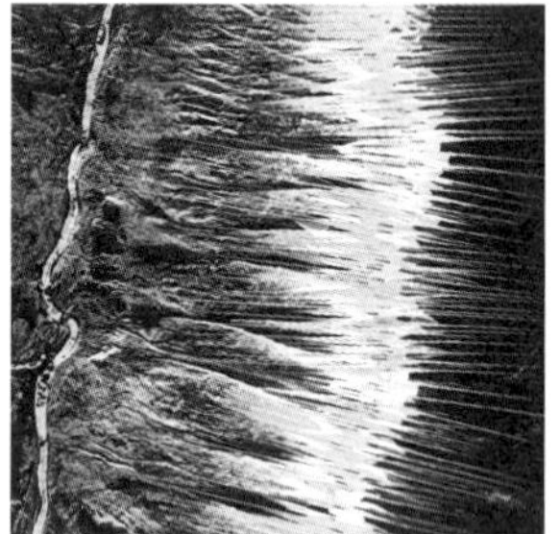

2.

3.

4.

4. View of exhausted mine entrances, 2056

5. Excavation robot blueprint, 2030

5.

6.

7.

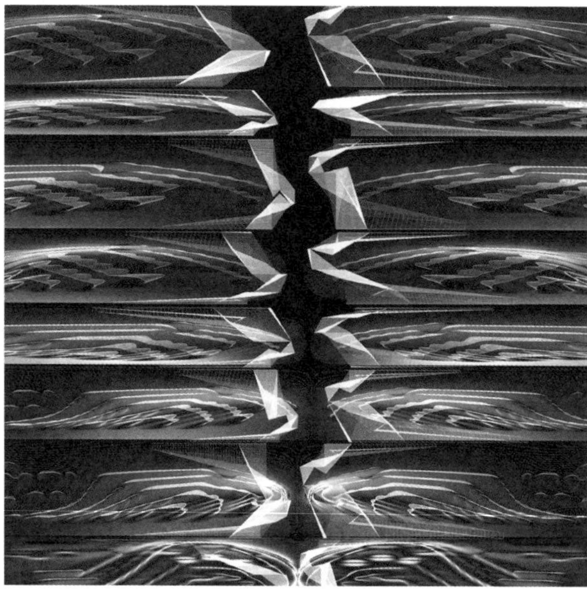

6. Model of razor-mine excavation chamber and terraform landscape

7. Topographic scan of terraformed excretions, 2031

STEPHEN MCNAMARA
The Hive: The Distribution of the Many

The tourist, yearning for an adventure but desperate for the peace of solitude, purchases a travel package for an Icelandic wilderness trip. Advertised as everyone's ideal form of touring, the trip will drop the visitors into the remoteness of Iceland, with a guarantee that they will not encounter one another.

The Icelandic Wilderness Experience was made possible only when, twenty years ago, a large investment was put toward the Wilderness Protection Plan to protect the image of Iceland. The Hive, the brain behind the park's daily operations, serves as the first prototype of what is now a building type for tourist distribution and monitoring.

Robotic in its motions, the building is tuned to sort, guide, and distribute users in isolation from the moment they land. A testament to its efficiency, one hundred tourists from Reykjavik can be funneled from a helicopter into individual accommodation pods in under ten minutes. There, once cleaned and equipped, the travel chamber is ready for inflating and subsequent occupation. Compressed air traveling from the pneumatic plant at the Hive's base is released into the pod mechanics and employed to propel the pods toward their predefined landing spot.

Exhausted upon his return, the visitor is surprised to find that the elevator does not open directly into his pod. Instead, the tourist is given a glimpse into the inner mechanics of the Hive; in fact, all the elevators open at different floors, each exposing hundreds of doors. The visitor finds himself at the center of a microcosmic-like gallery suspended inside the drum of the Hive. People congregate from every direction to share their adventures.

It's a party.

1. Image capture 20560713: inside gallery chandelier

2. The Hive, image capture 20560807: weekly launch trajectory mapping

1.

2.

3.

4.

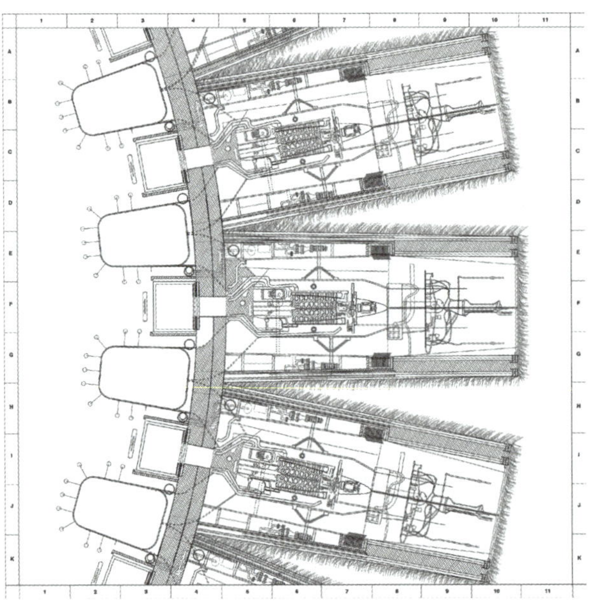

3. Image capture 20560725: returning to hive

4. The Hive (as built): typical plan of pod mechanics at rest

5. The Hive, image capture 20560807: weekly return-trail mapping

6. The Hive (as built): typical section of pod mechanics, extended

5.

6.

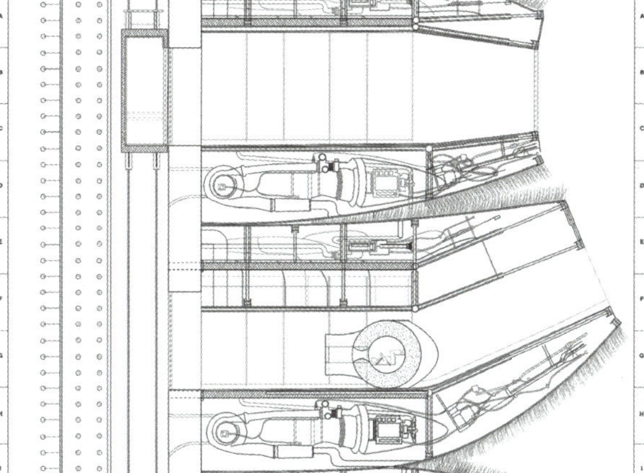

7.

8.

7. The Hive, image capture 20550522: elevation analysis

8. Model of Hive and pods

Image Credits

Young & Ayata: 4–5, 7, 8, 9; Harmen Brethouwer with Young & Ayata: 6; Heather Bizon: 12, 31 left, right, 32, 33 top, bottom, 34, 35 top, bottom left, bottom right; Robert Yoos: 13, 56, 57 top, bottom, 58, 59, 60 top, bottom; Heather Bizon and Paul Lorenz: 15 top; Matthew Bohne: 15 bottom, 41, 42 left, right, 43, 44, 45 top, bottom; Matthew Bohne, Robert Yoos, and Aymar Marino-Maza: 16 top; Cathryn Garcia-Menocal and Pauline Caubel: 16 bottom; Aymar Marino-Maza: 22 left, right, 23, 24, 25 top left, top right, bottom; Cathryn Garcia-Menocal: 26, 27, 28 top, bottom, 29 top, bottom, 30 top, bottom; Maggie Tsang: 37 top left, top right, bottom, 38, 39 top left, top right, bottom, 40 top, bottom; Paul J. Lorenz: 47 top, bottom, 48 top, bottom, 49, 50 top left, top right, bottom; Pauline Caubel: 51, 52 left, top right, top left, 53, 54, 55 top, bottom; Stephen Mcnamara: 61, 62 top, bottom left, bottom right, 63 top, bottom, 64 top, bottom.

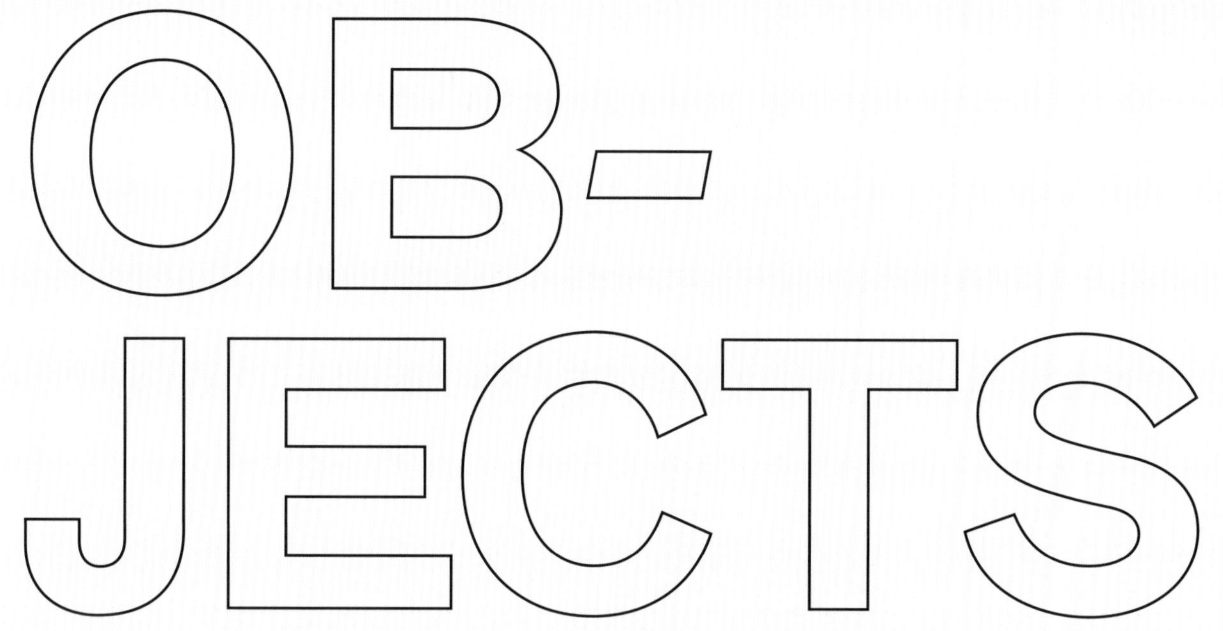

DAVID ERDMAN

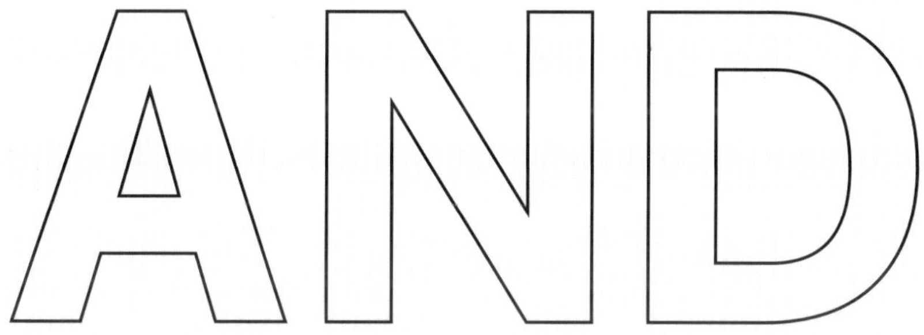

QUAL-
ITIES

**YALE
SCHOOL
OF
ARCHITECTURE**

**FUTURE
REAL**

**THE LOUIS I.
KAHN
VISITING
ASSISTANT
PROFESSORSHIP**

CON-
TENTS

IN-TER-VIEW

NINA RAPPAPORT
Servo, a network comprising architects Christopher Perry, Marcelyn Gow, and Ulrika Karlsson—did instrumental projects that weren't always constructed but were very much part of the architectural conversation. How has your work with them influenced you today?

DAVID ERDMAN
Servo took an anti-representational attitude to problems of modeling and drawing, largely through prototypical interventions in galleries, that was born out of the discourse on digital media and geometry. Our interests focused on how to work with various media. Projects incorporated light and sound—among other media, such as video—to produce environments that exceeded the scale of a physical object. Early work, like *thermocline* and *lattice archipelogics*, allowed us to study the effects of the environment on gallery visitors. The work was not client-based, allowing for an open-ended collaboration platform. The projects gave me a particular way to think about architectural intervention as a way of influencing space through the use of artificial lighting, sensors, color, sound, or motion.

NR Was it more of an experimental way to investigate new ideas stemming from available fabrication technologies?

DE This was our first five to eight years out of school, when those technologies were already starting to be questioned and pushed into alternative conceptual territory. It was what I refer to as the "after geometry" moment [named after Don Bates and Peter Davidson's "After Geometry" issue of *AD*], when essays such as Jeff Kipnis's "The Cunning of Cosmetics" and his exhibition Mood River—in which we participated—provided a disciplinary shift and consortium of venues, through the gallery, that opened a wide range of possibilities. When I started teaching at UCLA, discussions were intensifying about the concepts of "affect" and cosmetics, which I saw as pitted against traditional ideas of geometry and form. These shifted discussions premised upon a solely visual experience toward multisensorial experience, which galvanized my interests. In the work of servo, many projects were made of expendable, translucent plastic and robotically manufactured, thickened and materialized ephemeral media, creating temporal extensions of the physical object.

NR How did you decide to start the firm davidclovers with Clover Lee in Hong Kong, and how did you transition from servo to a more architectural practice?

DE I was interested in forming a different type of collaborative partnership that could test a range of audiences, including clients, and aggressively engage the city outside of the gallery. In early 2008, Clover and I decided to move to Hong Kong to explore the possibilities of working in the Pearl River Delta. Unexpectedly, I received the Rome Prize that year, and we detoured there en route to Hong Kong.

NR What was the subject of your Rome Prize research?

DE Stemming from a brief conversation with Mark Gage and Sylvia Lavin over a lunch break during the 2006 "Seduction" symposium at Yale, the project, called Plasticity Now, used Heinrich Wolfflin's book *The Renaissance and the Baroque*

Entrance to Clubhouse, part of The Repulse Bay complex alterations, Hong Kong, 2014. Courtesy plusClover.

Butterfly House, Poyntelle, Pennsylvania, 2014. Courtesy plusClover.

as its launching point. Understanding that the origins of architectural effects, as both discourse and design techniques, were born in Rome, I looked at four canonical buildings—San Carlo alle Quatro Fontane [Borromini], Sant'Andrea al Quirinale [Bernini], Palazzetto dello Sport [Nervi], and Villa La Serecena [Moretti]—and their common approach to plastic effects (embellishing how stone or plaster appeared fluid), their incorporation of other media, such as painting, frescoes, and sculpture, and/or how they could augment an environment through subtle, superficial moves. In retrospect, I can see how this provided a hinge between the work I did with servo and the work I did with davidclovers [now plusClover].

NR When you returned to practice, how were projects such as the Butterfly and Lunar houses influenced by your research?

DE One of the distinctive conceptual shifts Clover and I made was to focus on ideas of massing, which was an effort to move away from the "continuous surface" project. We incorporated counterintuitive ideas of mass media: massing media: slowing down that which is fast, and mass production, or producing mass: speeding up that which is slow. Both Lunar House and Butterfly House tapped into these ideas as a meditation on building enclosure and how it interacts with mass and its environment.

NR In what way is the surface graphic integrated as part of the 3-D architecture?

DE In Lunar House [unbuilt, but the façade prototype was exhibited in Immuring and reproduced for a Hong Kong storefront], we etched lines into the back-lit Corian façade so it would oscillate between something derived from the massing and something equally detached, depending on the time of day and pulsing of the lights. This produced a vertical lunar landscape, or fresco, that added an illusive depth to the suburban lot. Butterfly House took this to a different level, with vividly colored stainless-steel cladding increasing in intensity in the contoured areas of the mass. The neutral colors turn the corners along the profile or edge lines of the mass. The vibration between the coloration, massing, and enclosures produces an uncanny reversal of interior and exterior.

NR You also started to investigate the façade beyond the surface, in terms of making a mass out of the in-between space of a wall and expanding it to an occupied space. How do you feel that builds upon a new architecture and urbanism?

DE Yes, that was the shift in both projects, in that there is a degree of superficiality that simultaneously redefines the surfaces in favor of thickness and/or massing. My recent projects explore ideas of "objecthood"—a critically different yet affiliated interest with recent disciplinary trends in architectural objects. Many of them build upon the Lunar House projects and Butterfly House, containing significant concavity, or involution, and working within very tight, thin constraints. What is key is that they interact with a space that exceeds the perimeter of the physical object and, to a large extent, capture their adjacent void-spaces, engaging both urban and rural contexts.

NR Do you think that has the same effect as designing a full building in a tight, dense urban landscape, such as in Hong Kong, and how does it change your perception of urban interventions?

DE That is an important discussion. With regard to working in Asia and Hong Kong in particular, it is the pre-mirage of the twenty-first-century city, which is extremely dense and has a limited set of opportunities for ground-up building. So, the shift toward façades, concavity, and media is a response to urban pressure as well as opportunities to put pressure on existing disciplinary insecurities. There is a pejorative academic and professional attitude about doing interiors, façades, and the sort of alterations dominant in projects for dense, twenty-first-century cities.

NR But all of the great European architects who came to New York in the 1930s, such as Joseph Urban and Friedrich Kiesler, started by designing interiors, and even today it constitutes most urban commissions. How did you take the smaller urban project further by intervening in the housing estates in Hong Kong?

DE By not being so literal as to think that small objects operate only at the scale of their singular dimensions and by using various qualities—such as color, artificial light, and texture—to link these aspects together as cohesive experiences, not continuous geometries, by embracing the episodic intervention. We renovated a number of towers and podia for two separate Hong Kong housing estates: one was a complete gut renovation [part of the Repulse Bay Complex projects], and the other a façade renovation for a pair of towers [under construction now]. The projects episodically nip, tuck, and intervene in the estate, working together to engage void space and discontinuities as a collective alteration. These are object-like follies and individual rooms. They imbue a coarse sense of wholeness, cohesion, and pressure. This would not have been possible if I hadn't been part of servo, where we believed we could intervene in the context of the gallery without reconstructing it.

NR How do these projects relate to the idea of "objecthood" in contrast to "object-oriented ontology," which was the focus of a Yale conference last fall?

DE My interest in "objecthood" comes out of a particular reading of Michael Fried's essay "Art and Objecthood." The way I am defining it borrows heavily from disjunction and interventionist ideas, but without the "exploded field" interests. I am exploring the limit of how far apart objects can get before they detach, implying virtual continuities that fold back on themselves and become compact as wholes. I see this as an engagement with the void as much as with the physical artifact. This is latent within the sociopolitical understanding of housing estates, which give the residents an identity ["I live in Heung Fa Cheun"]. There is a linguistic articulation that reflects the fact that an estate is an urban "thing" with a discrete interior and exterior. Like Fried's analysis of a painting, somehow you still refer to that thing as one thing—yet housing estates are fields of objects.

NR What leeway were you given in the design of new insertions, and how did you approach the renovations from the interior to the building's infrastructure systems in Hong Kong projects?

DE Similar to New York City, Hong Kong has a major affordable-housing shortage. The Hong Kong Housing Authority is looking for densification models to address this and, at the same time, deal with the labor reductions and shortages forecast for the near future. The tower projects I have designed with davidclovers deploy significant amounts of prefabrication, address accelerated construction programs, and transform a standardized building into one with greater heterogeneity.

NR Do you believe the new condition of urban architecture—finding ways to squeeze construction into available space—needs to be acknowledged more broadly?

DE Well, I am personally more interested in building on top and within, rather than working with infill strategies and/or adjacencies. How we deal with spatial pressure as designers is very important, critically and professionally, as cities densify and ground-up work diminishes. Hong Kong is the only city currently operating at the levels of consumption the Paris Accord targeted for 2026, largely because of its density. Cities are beginning to grow more inward than outward. Among new design models are William Tsien's Asia Society, which kind of wrinkles around itself and interiorizes the landscape. The project is one part landscape, one part addition, one part conservation, and one part interior renovation. We have to grapple with those viscous mixtures

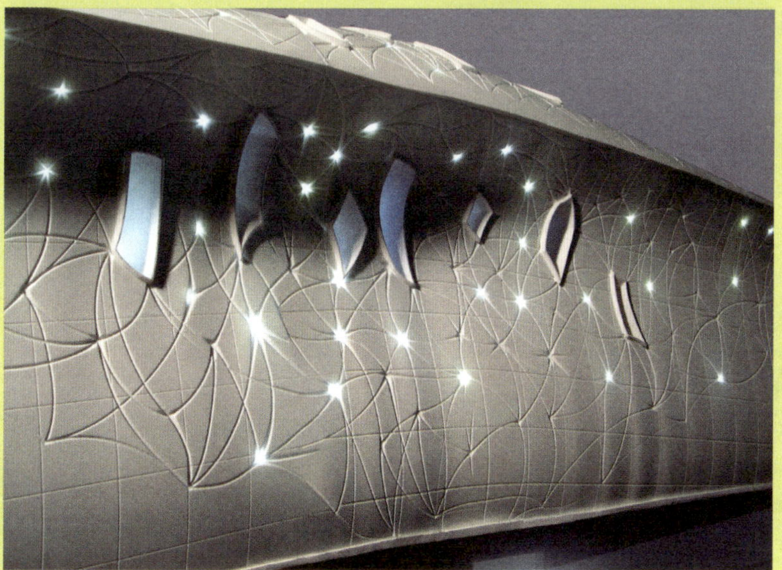

TOP Yud Yud, Commercial Storefront in Wan Chai, Hong Kong, 2004.
BOTTOM Model of Lunar House, Houston, Texas, 2008.
Both courtesy plusClover.

De Ricou Tower, Part of the The Repulse Bay Complex alterations, Hong Kong, 2013. Courtesy plusClover.

of disciplinarity, interior and exterior and part-to-whole. That is to a large extent what the studio at Yale will be addressing.

NR How will you teach this kind of approach to the students?

DE The studio, called "altered (e)states: objects and qualities," will speculate on fine-grained alterations as well as aggressive additions—atop the existing towers—using lightweight, prefabricated steel structures that will enable a roughly 30 percent increase in housing capacity. We will be looking at a multigenerational, two-key unit type. The HKHA wants younger people in its estates as both a value to the community and because they are the most economically disenfranchised, many of them living at home through their thirties and forties. The mix of units, compact singleton units and larger, multi-generational units, addresses a number of socioeconomic and infrastructural issues.

NR What made you want to return to the United States and apply for the Pratt Institute chair of the graduate programs? Do you have a new agenda for the school?

DE To a large extent, it was a perfect storm of circumstances for the Pratt position to transpire. As an architect, I believe it is important to approach everything as a designer. I am looking at how to embellish and nurture the existing potentials at Pratt, rather than demolish and start from the ground up. I guess you could call that an "alterationist" attitude.

ALT-ERED (E)-STAT-ES

ARCHITECTURE AND ITS INTERIORITY

If interiors are merely a category of professional work that occurs on the inside of buildings, "interiority" is the state of mind and perception induced by an architectural environment that is inwardly focused. An environment of this nature may have varying "degrees of interiority," but such a space is not limited to whether it is physically inside or outside of a building. Today, architects are increasingly considering the importance of interiority in urban centers as cities densify and how the discipline might shift its focus to include the alteration of various building environments. An understanding of architectural interiority has its roots in interior-design practice and goes against the mainstream of architectural education and practice. Interiors are conventionally designed in vignette-like formats that are understood as autonomous "rooms" and experienced as a series of episodes. Because interiors are disjointed from a building's exterior, their autonomous design contradicts five hundred years of architectural theory about part-to-whole relationships–the Holy Grail of the rules driving architecture.[1] In aggregate, these treatises and theories have repeatedly suggested, until the late twentieth century, that a building's exterior and interior need to be integrated and unified into an architectural whole.[2] Consequently, architects have seen the interior as being merely the other side of a building enclosure instead of seeing interiority as something that has immense potential.

Additional disciplinary and professional insecurities about the term *interiority*, let alone the embrace of interior-design principles is further clouded and contradicted by the practice of small, emerging firms in dense twenty-first-century cities. Young architects and architecture firms are often overtly biased toward ground-up work rather than interior-based work, suggesting an obsession with the architectural whole. In turn, this antiquated emphasis on part-to-whole architecture has hampered the development and execution of projects devoted to interiority. It can be challenging to see how that work is creative, bona fide career-building work when compared to ground-up projects that more directly re-assert architectural wholism. Thus, many emerging offices have been forced to seek work in faraway cities, such as the growing rural-urban centers in China or India or elsewhere, probing for a design market that offers opportunity to work on ground-up, whole buildings.

As populations increase, cities become denser, resources diminish, and economies constrict, architects will need to confront new methods of space-making. One could argue that the "topological" city, which prizes highly continuous, centrifugal qualities (and the economies and politics that drive them), is a rare and dying breed. In the not-so-distant future, city planners will have to consider (if they are not already) how to adapt and alter existing urban and architectural structures to grow inward and how to reconfigure their cities. This implies a necessary shift from the outward rings to inward thinking and opens the door to architects who can handle and be inventive with concepts of interiority. A snapshot across the globe shows these trajectories are already emerging in numerous cities, with competitions and awards increasingly involving adaptive-reuse projects.

A focus on interiority may subsequently be an essential conceptual element of the twenty-first-century architect's tool kit because it offers new ways to *alter* the perceptions of architectural environments within the context of contemporary urban and economic challenges, limited land use and densification being among two prevailing forces turning cities inward.[3] The concept of alteration, which is a aspect of inwardly growing, increasingly interiorized cities, could well be a game changer for nimble, experimentally oriented architecture firms, allowing them to contribute in new, market-savvy ways to adaptive-reuse projects. The emergence and increasing prevalence of alterations and additions work, which tend to limit an architect's scope to only the exterior or the interior, is the type of work that most contemporary practices must take on if they want to engage the city.

Two projects that signal both theoretical and practical opportunities within this type of work are located in Hong Kong—globally one of the densest cities—and designed and executed by two firms that have embraced architectural interiority: Tod Williams/Billie Tsien Architects and Partners' Asia Society Hong Kong Center and Herzog & de Meuron's Police Central Headquarters share interventionist tactics, and both practices seem comfortable spanning the gamut between ground-up construction, conservation, landscape, and interiors.

It is important to point out the attributes of Hong Kong that harness and magnify issues of interiority and its productive potential. Unlike most contemporary Asian cities, Hong Kong experienced its growth period more than sixty years ago. Now possessing a mature, highly dense building fabric, it is one of the most expensive regions in the world in which to build, making land use and development challenging.[4] Built out, episodic, layered, and interiorized, Hong Kong is more typical of a twenty-first-century city than of a late-twentieth-century city, which may be described as being open, smooth, continuous, and free to grow outward, typically in concentric, ring-like formations. On the other hand, Hong Kong and similar twenty-first-century cities, amplify the discord between exterior and interior conditions more so than do twentieth-century cities because they are so dense and folding back in on itself. Indeed, the twenty-first-century city's interior and exterior spaces may be entirely different from and at odds with one another. Driven largely by the desire to minimize risk by involving more than one designer, style, and brand, contemporary development and financing found in Hong Kong and other similar cities calls for this opposition, as do project briefs. Architecture contracts are, more often than not, separated from interior-design contracts. These legal and financial trends perpetuate environments that are intentionally and architecturally unresolved in their part-to-whole relations.[5]

Thus, the perception of a twenty-first-century city's interiority contrasts with the perception of its exteriority. One could extend the analysis even further by drawing a correlation between the psyche of the contemporary urban subject, whose highly mediated and constructed exterior (think Instagram, Facebook) is in stark contrast to what they know of themselves or perhaps their many selves. The twenty-first-century city and its inhabitant subjects may no longer anticipate nor desire part-to-whole relations or their gestalt resolution. If anything, one could go so far as to speculate that the thirst for urbanity that is driving populations to move into cities could be precisely a desire for this discordant texture of experiences, a desire that has not gone unrecognized by the building industry's financial and marketing departments. Learning from Hong Kong, we might predict that the future city will no longer harbor the compulsion to smooth out the topologies of interior and exterior or resolve part-to-whole relationships. Instead, architectural design will have to find new spaces of practice. A possibility is that architectural interiority, because it produces a tension between interior and exterior where they are related but

TOP Asia Society Hong Kong Center, Admiralty Hong Kong, 2012, Tod Williams Billie Tsien Architects, aerial photograph of the Asia Society complex showing new and existing structures, renovated structures layered atop and beside one another. Photograph by © Michael Moran/OTTO.
BOTTOM Central Police Station Compound, Central Hong Kong, under construction, Herzog & de Meuron. Rendering showing one of two infill intervention-additions atop and surrounded by renovated existing structures that articulate the corner of the courtyard. View from within the courtyard. Courtesy © Herzog & de Meuron.

not the same. This opens up opportunities to give disparate environments a degree of a cohesion and interiority. Engaging the practices and milieu that force concepts of interiority into the realm of architecture necessitates an embrace of alteration, a word and subject worthy of deeper examination.

ALTERATION

The mid- to late-twentieth-century obsession with digital technology often relied on biological models to resolve how architecture can adapt to its changing context. This approach could be applied to both the interior and exterior spaces of architecture, from the endlessness of Kiesler to the metabolic capacities of architecture as seen, for instance, in Japan.[6] While some notable advances in this subject have manifested in a host of formal, parametric, and geometric experiments, it is difficult to ignore the role of adaptation in the profession through ideas of adaptive reuse. Used more often as a marketing ploy than a conceptual opportunity, adaptation is ripe, however, for theoretical expansion and tectonic interrogation, particularly in relation to ideas of interiority. For the most part, architectural adaptation projects are conceived from the ground up, introducing a comprehensive and whole architectural system into a project's context. The contemporary field of architectural software favors this continuous, smooth, singular, and fully integrated approach. Alteration projects, on the other hand, open up fresh discursive territory that builds upon the ideas of adaptation by affronting standardization, perhaps with a few distinctions. The alteration route is somewhat more restrained, fine-grained, and interiorized. More centripetal than centrifugal in its design strategies, alteration pulls and tucks a structure into shape, rather than deforming it to adjust to adjacencies.

Because of alteration's episodic characteristics, its strategies are not only in line with the emerging qualities of twenty-first-century cities like Hong Kong but also open up the potential to reconsider the theories of disjunctive or fragmented architectures that gained acceptance in the eighties.[7] To a large extent, those theories are absent from digital architecture today due to an obsession with continuity and an intellectually stubborn insistence on designing the whole. From a post-digital perspective, however, disjunctive theories offer a limit for testing adaptive strategies. To what extent do alteration and an emphasis on interiority allow the discipline to rethink the architectural whole? Can strategies of alteration be pushed close to the disjunctive extreme of fragmentation while maintaining enough cohesion to be understood as forming new types of architectural wholes? Does alteration allow for a way to engage new ways of thinking that embrace, rather than exile, interiority-based architecture?

OBJECTHOOD AND CENTRIPETAL QUALITIES

Issues of interiority and the subject of alteration might become central to the work of many contemporary architects, as noted earlier. To a large extent, the necessity to enlarge a theoretical framework and creatively engage each related subject may arise out of the circumstances of contemporary practice. Increasingly, architecture practice in dense cities takes on projects that have a non-traditional scope, involving one part architecture, one part interior design, one part conservation, one part landscape, and/or one part product design. It is equally important to seek out ways to theorize these types of opportunities while working to understand them within the context of their urban landscapes.

The studio at Yale, "altered estates: objects and qualities," was a guiding point toward architectural interiority foregrounding strategies of alteration and densification in Hong Kong. It is important to recall that when discussing the architectural whole, we are effectively talking about its qualities; its degrees of comprehensive "objecthood."[8] Architecture is rarely if ever made from one monolithic and/or solid "object" without an interior. Historically, architects have considered architectural objects (meaning, assemblies with particular qualities) as fully integrated entities: interior and exterior, structure and skin, and so on.[9] Objecthood is one way to begin to frame a discourse that allows for both the fragmentary and the cohesive, the existing and new, the interior and exterior, to co-exist in compressed formations of void space. The "hood" in "objecthood" is key to this, and the concept was central to the studio at Yale.

If Hong Kong's density allows one to explore new understandings of objects (objecthood), it also tests one's ingenuity to alter, foregrounding a second qualitative attribute important to the studio: centripetality. As an incredibly dense and pressurized city, Hong Kong has little room to stretch out (partly for financial reasons found in GFA calculations and partly for physical reasons); there simply is not enough space or land.[10] Alteration is a productive, if not obvious way into rethinking the potentials of Hong Kong. We can summarize architectural alteration as exercises that are adjusting select, disjointed areas, not an entire original object. Its reinvigorated use within the studio staged a set of possibilities that might be generally understood as seeking out ways to pull experience inward rather than exuberantly showing off the object's qualities on the visible, prioritized exterior. The use of minor and major forms of involutions, from subtle, concave façades to deep, thick, figured interiors, constituted a range of key methods students used to spin the context inward and foreground "interiorized space objects" and their centripetal qualities. The inwardly focused centripetal concept is an ingenious tactic for operating in dense cities and allows "space objects" to emerge with a semi-autonomy from traditional architecture's casing, enforcing episodic and interventionist characteristics. The Yale students' work offers an opportunity to understand how interiorized space objects can be disparate but simultaneously working to form a cohesive landscape. The studio examined the immense operative and theoretical potential for altering a test-case program within Hong Kong: public rental housing estates. The studio's ensemble of projects pushed the limits of the concepts previously outlined in this essay and the scale at which they might be deployed. The results were astounding, with each student project manifesting a different set of concerns within the same framework.

In many ways, alteration is a call to be more resourceful as designers. There is the obvious advantage of recycling an existing building fabric and limiting the resources of development, both of which underscore the opportunities in the PRH estates. Alteration may also unleash other types of resources, from the conceptual to the experiential. Learning from the disjunctive theories of the eighties and transforming them in new, innovative ways, including the direct embrace of interiority and its objecthood, allows room to build architectural resources and bring into Architecture's scope of work that is in danger of being done by other designers and/or pejoratively and arrogantly tossed to the side as unworthy of an architect's attention. Architectural practices need to embrace the realities of the cities in which they practice and, at the same time, speculate on how to transform them, which, as this essay has attempted to argue, would require us to reconceive our understanding of the architectural whole and concepts of interiority.

Experimenting with the limits of continuity and fragmentation through alteration allows for a greater degree of compatibility with existing architectural systems, as well as an even greater plurality of experience and effect. In this context, the Yale studio and its sites served as an interesting testing ground to use alteration concepts to augment a heterogeneity of experience through diverse environments, material assemblies, and moods, while producing enough cohesion to give the estates a new identity. Alteration can be seen as a way to resituate interiority in architecture, highlighting disjunctive capacities of new types of wholes and new types of objects while ushering in post-digital themes relevant to the academy and cultural trends. If we can employ alteration to rethink the architectural whole, the future of interiority and its related praxes may open up fertile speculative realities.

Portions of this essay appeared in *The Architecture Theory Reader,* Ed. Gregory Marinic (Routledge 2018).

FOOTNOTES

1. The *Interior Architecture Reader* is one of the first readers to focus on interiors. See also Mark Taylor (ed.) and Julieanna Preston (ed.), *Intimus: Interior Design Theory Reader* (New York: Wiley, 2006) and Lois Weinthal, *Toward a New Interior* (New York: Princeton Architectural Press, 2011).

2. From Vitruvius's *Ten Books on Architecture* (c.1500) to Le Corbusier's *Vers Une Architecture* (1923), the architectural whole is reasserted as a primary goal for the beauty, function, and pleasure of architectural design. When the Smithsons critiqued wholism in the 1950s, the ideas of fragmentary and disjointed cities emerged. Readers include Joan Ockman, *Architecture Culture 1948–68* (New York: Columbia Books of Architecture, 1993) and K. Michael Hays's sequel *Architecture Theory Since 1968* (New York: MIT Press, 1998).

3. See *United Nations Department of Economic and Social Affairs World Urbanization Report, 2014 Revision*, http://esa.un.org/unpd/wup/Highlights/WUP2014-Highlights.pdf; see also United Nations DESA Development Policy and Analysis Division "World Economic Situation and Prospects" report at www.un.org/en/development/desa/policy/wesp/.

4. Hong Kong's population increase occurred from 1931 to 1961, roughly forty to fifty years earlier than Shenzhen's, Beijing's, or Shanghai's (Sources: Figure 1, Wendell Cox, "The Evolving Urban Form: Hong Kong," *New Geography*, 2012, www.newgeography.com/content/002708-the-evolving-urban-form-hong-kong. See also Figure 3, Wendell Cox, "Pakistan: Where the New Population Bomb Is Exploding," *New Geography*, 2012, www.newgeography.com/content/002940-pakistan-where-population-bomb-exploding), making it among the most mature modern cities in China. It is the third-densest region in the world (Source: UN Demographia: "Population Density" chart) and the most expensive city to build in (Sources: EC Harris and Langdon & Seah, 2013, "International Cost Comparison" chart ranking the average cost of construction).

5. This practice is common even among the top developers in Hong Kong, like Swire or Hong Kong Shanghai Hotels, both of which are distinguished by their devotion to design. Also they have worked with notable architects and interior designers such as Frank Gehry, Kengo Kuma, and Peter Marino. Tenders are increasingly broken up in this manner, which is in part a democratic effort to spread the wealth to the design community (and not bias any one practice), evident in recent Urban Renewal Authority projects, and capitalizes on a spectrum of markets and styles within any one property, especially in residential housing estates. The Pacific Century Premium Development's Bel-Air on the Peak development, in Pok Fu Lam, is an example that shifts from faux neo-baroque interiors to the sleek, curvilinear modernity of Norman Foster's Bel-Air No.8.

6. See Friedrick Kiesler's Endless House project (1950) and the Nakagin Capsule Tower (1972) by Kisho Kurokawa, which use biological adaptation to underpin their form, geometry, and massing.

7. See the MoMA 1988 *Deconstruction*, Aldo Rossi's *Architecture and the City* (Institute for Architecture and Urban Studies and MIT, 1982) and Bernard Tschumi's *Architecture and Disjunction* (MIT Press, 1996). The benefit of looking back at this work after twenty years of smooth and continuous digital projects is to embrace the agility of the fragment and the disjunctive while trying to explore how those interventions do not remain entirely separate follies but, instead, form new types of more-complex architectural wholes.

8. See Michael Fried, "Art and Objecthood" (*Art Forum 5*, June 1967, Jonathan Edwards), understand the architectural object. Fried's definition of "objecthood" is distinguishable from speculative realism and object oriented ontology as a predominately perceptual and sensual idea within the practices and aesthetics of art, more directly aligned to architecture and its potential praxes when compared with Graham Harmon's Triple O, Meillasoux, and philosophical discussions of Kant's object of knowledge.

9. Ockman, *Architecture Culture* 1948–68; Hays *Architecture Theory since 1968*. See endnote No. 2.

10. Ground-floor-area calculations limit the economy of Hong Knog buildings, which tend to prioritize the monetization of floor-plate areas over design. As such, one sees an intensively Fordist production of housing throughout the city and over many decades limiting the extent to which architects can "branch out." While Hong Kong occupies only one-third of its total land area, the remaining two-thirds are seen as both an asset and economically unfeasible to develop. They provide the city with a robust network of country parks and recreation but are difficult to develop due to their steep terrain. Ongoing debates about whether to release this land for development continue; however, they are unlikely to resolve themselves in a sea change of land releases, reasserting the idea that Hong Kong has very little land to build upon.

Objects and objecthood are heavily debated, multidimensional subjects within the discipline of architecture, which has seen reinvigorated interest in them among a number of designers and thinkers in the past two years. Some of the intention behind this renewed interest is to openly and frankly admit that architects are hired to design objects, that we are good at designing them, and that we have expertise about them that other disciplines do not share. "Objects and Qualities" was also interested to redefine objects and understand them within the broader context of objecthood.

Many architects see objects as a deficient, short-sighted, and limited "state" of architecture. At the turn of the century, obsession with fields, voids, and scales, particularly those scales that are presumed to exceed the "singular" object, reinforced the idea that objects are not what architects design, nor should they be designing them. However, defining the limits of objects may not be as simple as one presumes, and there may be a number of productive outcomes for both the profession and the discipline that result from an intensive re-examination of objects, objecthood, and their related definitions. This position is what formed the launching point of the "Objects and Qualities" studio, which exposed students to counterintuitive understandings of architectural objects that emphasized their fragmentary capacities and how those objects may alter their contexts.

Public rental housing estates were the focus of the studio. Students examined how to alter and redefine them. Housing estates were an important test case because they nicely encapsulate one of the primary contradictions surrounding the subject of objecthood: how can a collection of four to forty buildings be referred to as one thing (an estate)? Is it a single object or a collection or field of objects? The studio experimented with aspects of objecthood principally by emphasizing material qualities as they relate to objects. Students explored the limits of objecthood by altering the intrinsic and extrinsic qualities of housing blocks, their façades, and the estates at large. Working with past and present members of the Hong Kong Housing Authority, and internationally renowned façade consultants as well as visiting Hong Kong, the students were exposed to the discursive, sociopolitical, local, regional, and international aspects of how to innovatively attack, as design architects, one small piece of the overall "housing problem" in Hong Kong.

The studio was modeling-intensive. Physical models were the primary "objects" the students used to design and study the material qualities. The majority of the work was done via study models and hyper-realistic photographic montages.

View showcasing compression of space surrounding typical Hong Kong housing block as well as the coarse texture and hatching of the crenelated facade. Courtesy David Erdman.

TEST-CASE BACKGROUND

Hong Kong is among the most mature cities in Asia, among the most dense territories in the world, and among the most expensive to build upon due to its limited land supply. It also is a city that urgently must come to terms with its housing shortage. The Long-Term Housing Strategy (LTHS), formulated in 2013 and updated in 2015, laid out a broad set of goals to deal with public housing in Hong Kong. The concept of altering objects and, specifically, housing estates, using suggestions directly from the LTHS report, framed the studio as students looked at strategies to build atop existing public rental housing (PRH) estates and comprehensively renovate existing façades. Using lightweight, advanced construction techniques and a lightweight composite façade system of ceramic tile, the studio's goal was to maximize the mass and density of housing while minimizing the impact on existing communal space, fresh air, and daylight. The studio used as its site of experimentation the reinforced-concrete superstructures found in many PRH estates.

In 2013, the Hong Kong Housing Authority, which oversees Hong Kong's public housing estates, developed the LTHS report to deal with the limited supply of affordable public rental housing and the limited supply of land available to address the housing demand. Three factors defined the studio: the LTHS report, the history of construction practices for PRH projects of a certain period, and the broader implications of how architects may come to redefine architectural objects and their qualities at a certain scale.

Specifically, the LTHS document suggests that a study be conducted to seek out those estates in which the GFA (ground-floor area) is low enough to permit building in between the existing buildings. While this tactic is an innovative way to address the limited supply of housing in Hong Kong, the solution comes at the expense of existing residents in PRH estates where highly valuable daylight, fresh air, viewing corridors, and communal areas would be compromised or obstructed. The focus of the studio was to explore intensive architectural design and engineering methods of altering these estate tower-objects that would simultaneously increase the quantity of housing and minimize its impact on the existing resources of the site.

The construction industry in Hong Kong is historically behind international standards for its use of sustainable materials, advanced engineering methods, and fabrication. This is most evident in the public-housing sector, less so in private housing, and even less so in commercial, infrastructural, and civic projects. Furthermore, the Hong Kong government forecasts significant construction labor shortages in the short and long term, due to immigration and labor-policy adjustments between mainland China and Hong Kong. Thus, PRH projects are in dire need of being brought up to these construction standards and innovative practices to address a multitude of issues the Hong Kong Housing Authority is facing. Many PRH tower-blocks contain robust superstructures. Based on prior research with Arup and Front, it was estimated that the collection of PRH tower-block estates built in the eighties and nineties were resilient enough to

View from roof top "elevated podium" level of one of the Hong Kong housing estates students studied and toured in the New Territories. Courtesy David Erdman.

Multilevel interior void (space object) of an existing Hong Kong housing estate students studied for its sectional qualities.

take some additional weight—that is, to subtract or add mass at the top. The tower-blocks comprising these estates are reinforced-concrete construction and use shear-wall designs to form their superstructure, allowing students to speculate on tactics that employ a minimum amount of new structure to be scabbed or stitched atop or in front of the existing building.

DISCIPLINARY BACKGROUND

The idea of alteration has great potential in the future of architectural thinking and already has begun to reconfigure and assert new conceptions and definitions of the architectural object or, more specifically, qualities of architectural objecthood. One can locate conceptual and stylistic threads of thinking that relate to alteration in the discipline as recently as the late eighties and early nineties in, for example, Bernard Tschumi's *Architecture and Disjunction*. Largely theoretical in nature, Tschumi's texts and theories make an effort to distinguish a disjunctive "language" of architecture from an architecture that is singular or whole. Until that moment in the late twentieth century, the mainstream of the history of architecture largely focused on how to design a more beautiful, integrated, whole building. The notions of infill architecture and parasitic architectures are certainly nothing new to the discourse, and there have been some stunning projects in the past ten years that test the limits of these ideas. The studio built upon this emerging platform of work and ideas as a means of pushing the envelope of alteration. It challenged the students to negotiate and creatively alter existing architectural objects and their related qualities.

Object-oriented ontology, a strain of philosophy spearheaded by Graham Harman, is among the recent theoretical ideas that have captured the attention of numerous architects. Building upon ideas of speculative realism and critiquing earlier philosophers' understanding of different types of objects and how subjects receive and perceive them (like Kant's "objects of knowledge"), these philosophers believe that objects cannot be fully understood or designed. Object-oriented ontology sees an object's qualities as elusive and mysterious, resulting in deep levels of interaction and cognition between the human subject and the object.

While Triple O (the slang for object oriented ontology) is an invaluable advance on the discourse of architectural objects, it is perhaps too limited in scope and narrow in its resultant architectural translation to date. Accusations of architects being nostalgic for the "pure object" or trying to "mystify" the design process and its outputs form the counterpoint to these interests. In order to sidestep some of the ways in which objects are currently being theorized via Triple O and avoid some of the emerging latent and explicit criticisms of this approach toward advancing the discourse on architectural objects, the issue of alteration bares great potential and the subject of objecthood is perhaps even more critical. Building upon Michael Fried's seminal article "Art and Objecthood," the studio takes the position that objecthood is a quality or affect of objects that necessarily involves the use of voids and fields. This specific understanding of objects and objecthood activates both fields and voids as alternative forms of objects. In adopting this premise and using the intrinsic density of the altered housing estates to pressurize the space between existing and new buildings and between tower-blocks, the studio yielded an opportunity to experiment with "space-objects," further articulating them with intense, materially vivid qualities. This approach allowed the students to theorize the spaces between existing and new, and between the building blocks of an estate itself as well as examine their fragmented and contradictory, yet collective, degrees of objecthood. They could also examine their specifically selected estate's fragmented and contradictory, yet collective, degrees of objecthood via their alterations and those alteration's qualities.

Detailed model photograph of two textural facade types accentuating the qualities of the proposed space object emerging from the interior at the corner of the housing block addition atop the existing tower.

STUDIO METHOD AND ORGANIZATION

The studio was organized into two principle areas of research: objects and qualities. The case studies' existing superstructures were understood as a new type of ground and site upon which the students could excavate, alter, and add new structures. In the first part of the semester, which focused on the definition of objects, the students worked from the interior to the exterior. In the semester's second part, which focused on those object's qualities and relationships, the students worked from the exterior to the interior. Working individually and then in teams of two, the students honed options for individual tower-block types. In the third part of the semester, each team focused on how to cultivate both the fragmentary and object-like qualities of the tower-blocks and the estates at large.

The semester foregrounded the development of geometrical systems to establish innovative relationships with the existing structure. This open-ended, somewhat abstract experiment emphasized semi-autonomous relationships between existing and new. As the semester progressed, students focused on structure and organization. Using a fixed primary construction system of prefabricated lightweight steel in conjunction with a secondary prefabricated enclosure system of glass-fiber reinforced-concrete (GRC) cladding and ceramic tile, students tested their initial massing concepts. Teams focused on how to develop efficient unit layouts within the new structure and how to establish strong connections to the existing building. Circulation, structure, and program acted on geometry and mass, and the geometry and mass were studied with an eye toward their reciprocity. Overall, the models, initial test studies, and ideas from the first part of the semester were brought to fruition in the semester's second part.

A housing workshop and field trip to Hong Kong were topped off with visits to the five housing estates the students were studying as well as discussions and seminars with various stakeholders and experts, including Stephen Yim (chief architect of the Hong Kong Housing Department), Michael Ra and Martin Reise (principals, and Evan Levelle Associate Principal, Front Inc., Hong Kong), Christopher Webster (dean of Hong Kong University's faculty of architecture), Nasrine Saraji (head of Hong Kong University's department of architecture), and Rebecca Chiu (head of Hong Kong University's department of planning). Marc Simmons (principal of Front Inc., New York City) led two technical workshops and focused on the structural, environmental, and façade aspects of each team's proposal.

Students worked with physical models throughout the semester. Models and photography were favored over rendering. Models were executed using mixed media, including 3-D prints, laser-cutting elements, and hand-cut elements.

STU-
DENT
PROJ-
ECTS

GRO-UND UP

ILANA SIMHON AND
BRITTANY OLIVARY

Challenging the typical notion of ground-up construction, this project defines the skyline of Hong Kong as a new ground zero. With no room to expand outward, this project's idea of ground-up construction seeks to remedy the housing crisis by building atop the current tower-blocks. The new construction is made feasible by the robust concrete sheer-wall construction used in the existing towers, allowing for the new communities to be read as objects that redefine the urban fabric. Beginning as the Harmony 1 Cruciform block type, *(Ground) Up* transforms this typology into an objectified courtyard bounded by a double-L of housing. The amenity space that fills the courtyard weaves between two blocks, producing a cross-block cadence and linking two communities into one. The units that occupy the double-L respond to the surroundings and, consequently, take on characteristics of sidedness to challenge the current conditions of relentless repetition. From the exterior, the tower-block adapts the original scale of the punched openings to make a double skin at the upper levels. This tactic works to obscure the conventional reading of a housing tower. As *(Ground) Up* forms a new terrain in the sky, it latches onto the existing block and re-originates the housing estate at large.

Street view

Corner
OPPOSITE Cross-block relationship

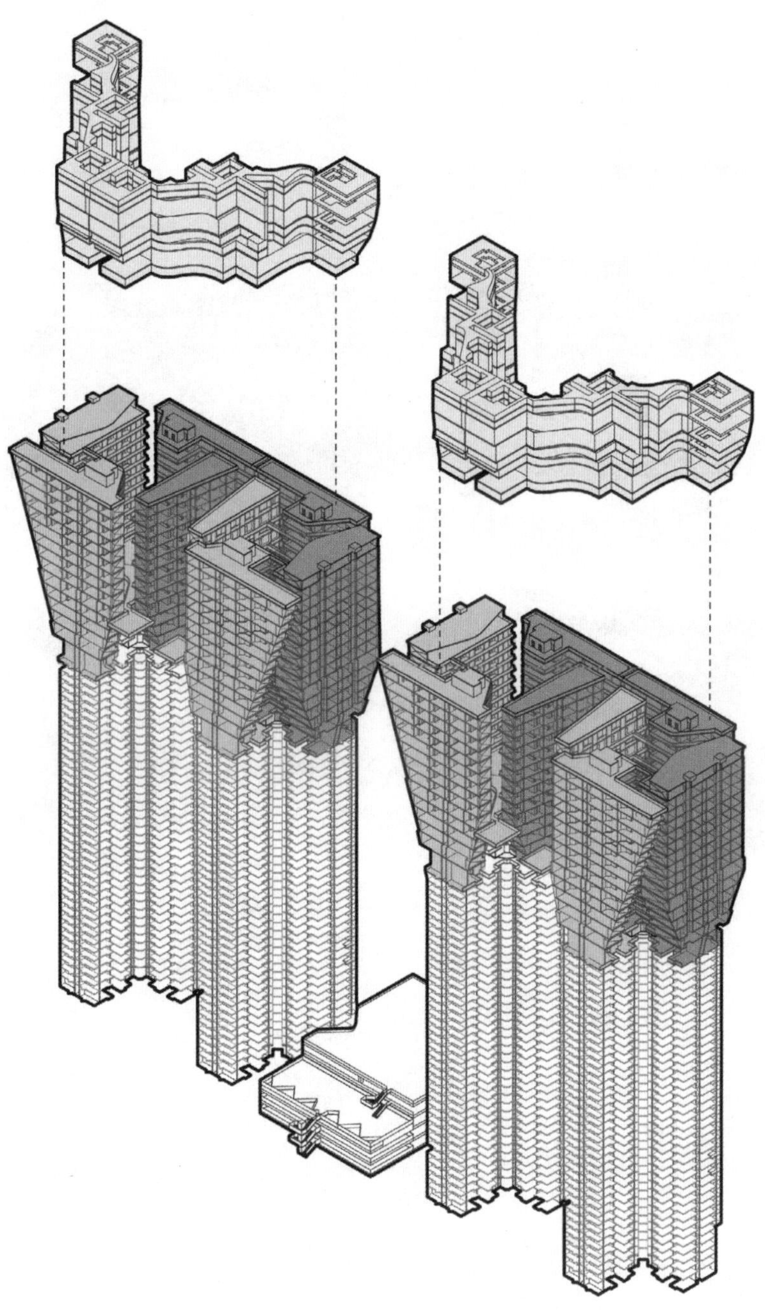

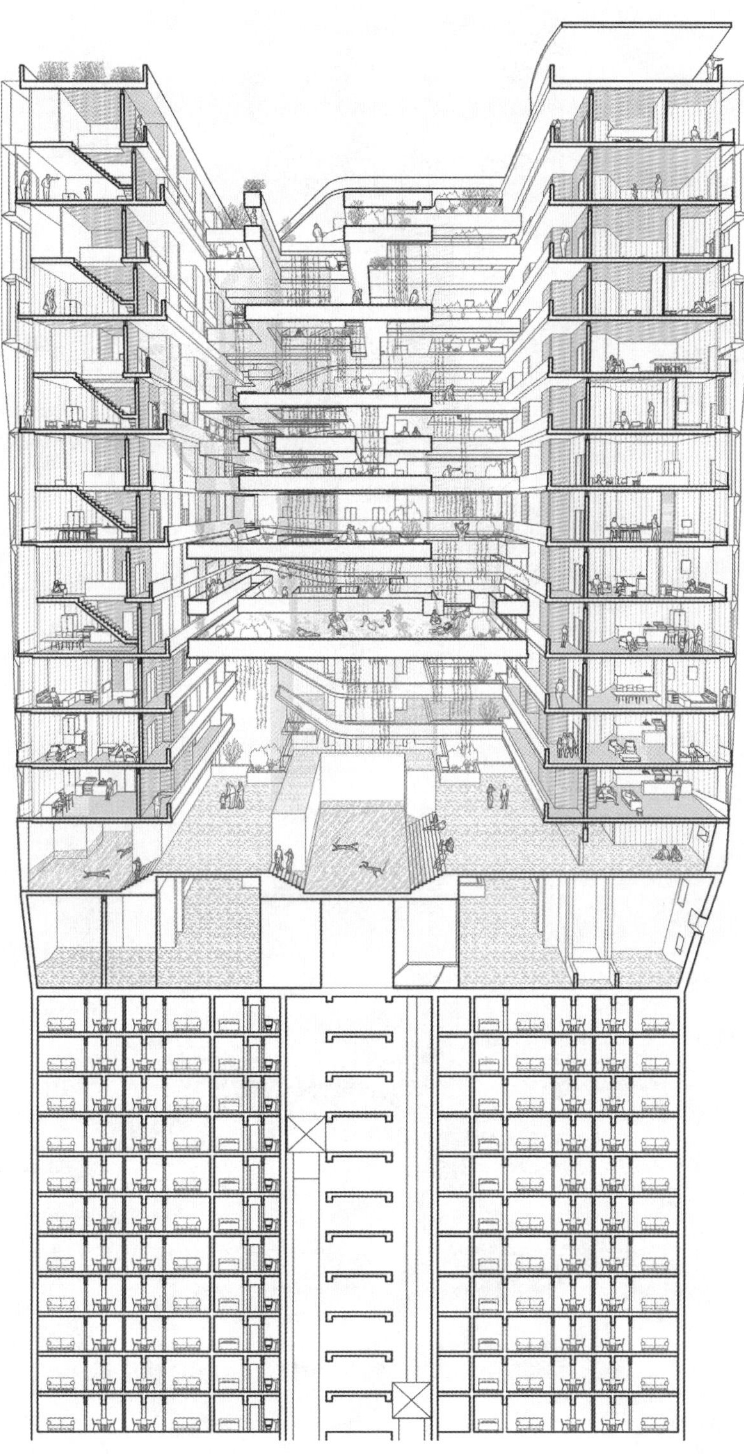

Section
OPPOSITE Tsz Man estate site model

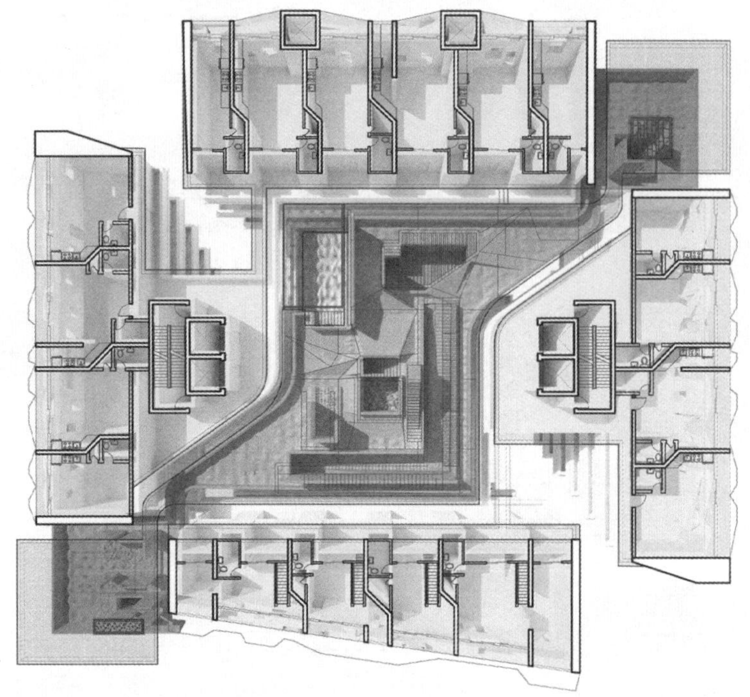

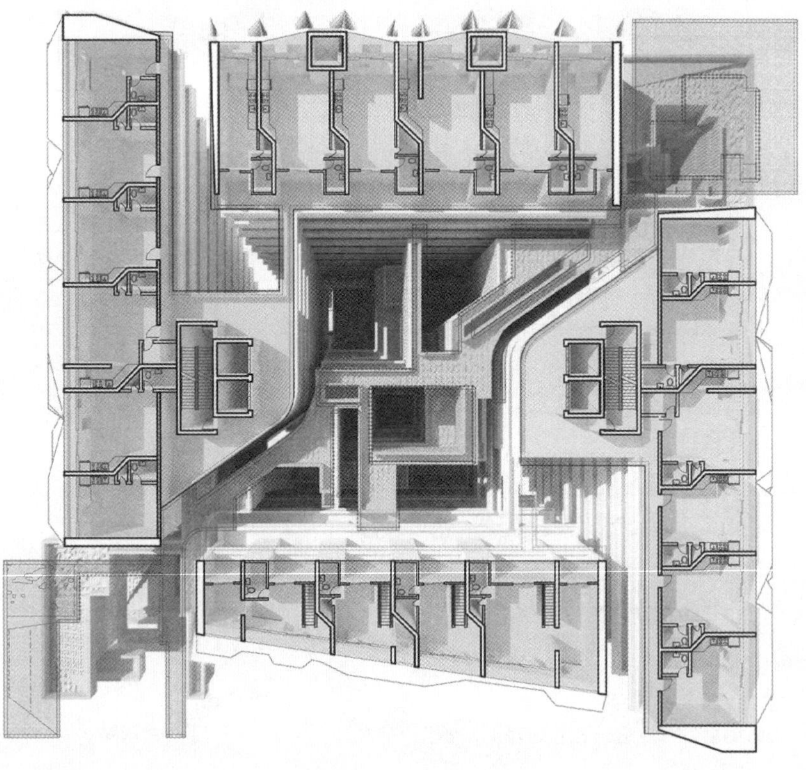

Aerial view
OPPOSITE Plans from mid-level units (top) and upper-level units (bottom)

Model shot
OPPOSITE Reflexology landscape

Exterior façade obscures the single unit

Nighttime shot of façade

LEE ON CAN-OPY

ROB CORNELLISON AND
JOLANDA DEVALLE

The motivation behind this project's addition is to provide more amenities for each apartment by increasing the tower's density. Here, pockets of space are internalized within the exterior form of the existing tower, a typical gesture of Hong Kong's housing estates.

The resulting open-air voids penetrate the addition to make private courtyards for each unit, providing a closer connection to nature and enabling an expanded floor plate for more air and light. The voids also provide seamless structural integrity, acting as large columns that take the gravitational load of the new addition. While the plan remains incredibly dense, each unit's three exterior sides create the sense of being close to nature and wide-open space. While the courtyard within each apartment is a private amenity at the top of the building, each void merges into a single, open exterior space in the center. A façade of louvres provides optimal shading while changing the texture of what is clearly an addition in the daytime to the feeling of porosity at night.

Interior model shot
OPPOSITE TOP Daytime view of exterior
OPPOSITE BOTTOM Nighttime rendering

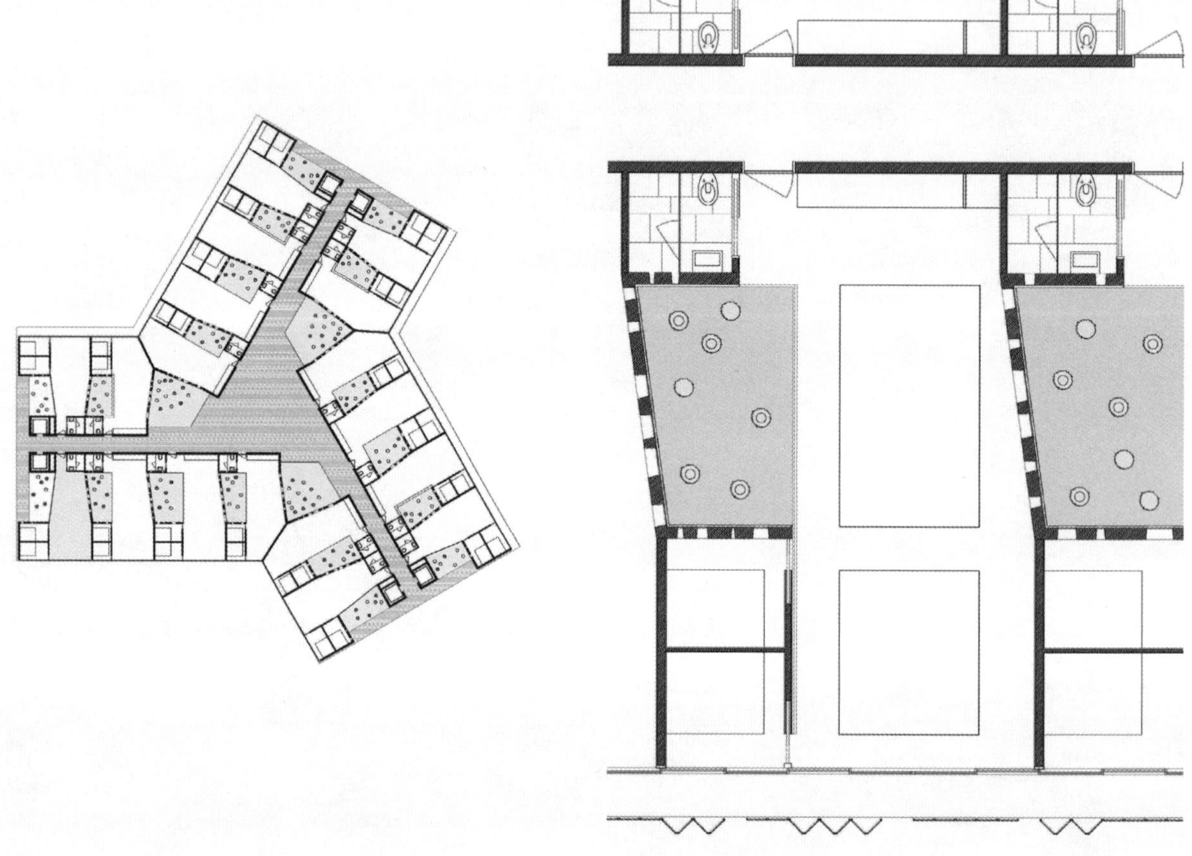

Plans
OPPOSITE Detail shot of façade

Aerial view of site

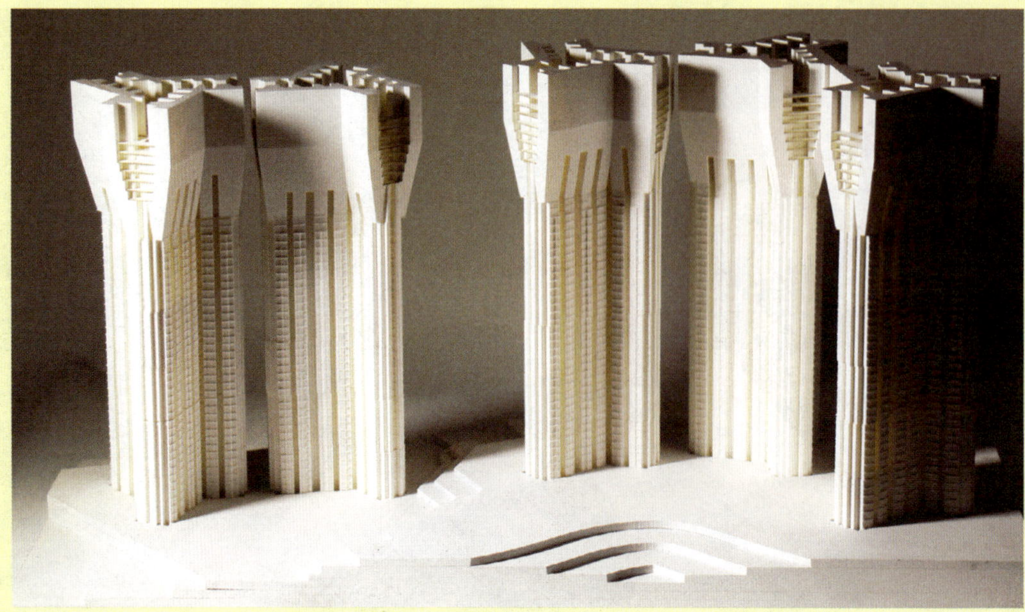

TOP Physical model
BOTTOM Model
OPPOSITE Rendering of exterior from street view

Estate from back

INTO THE VOID

FRANCESCA CARNEY
CECILY NG
AJIN RYU

Offering an addition to a public housing estate, this project brings the highly textural qualities of the existing Hong Kong built landscape to the proposed buildings' interior. The skin of the three tower-blocks at Shek Yam East transforms them into one building. Within each tower addition, cracks at the corners activate sidedness at the scale of the estate, and a central void reveals the texture within.

Texture on the interior creates semi-public zones that extend to amenities that can be used by residents for their own temporary use. Residential life expands out into the central void, increasing dwelling space in a very dense city.

Brick-like perforations break down the monolithic exterior at a smaller scale and serve to screen private balconies for every unit. They provide shade and privacy, two valuable amenities in Hong Kong. Foreseeing increased density, views are focused up and down, rather than horizontally.

The additions form multiple gateways into the estate and connect the urban zone to the park that borders Shek Yam East. Contrasting a monolithic exterior with a textured interior, the additions create interiority at the scale of the block and the estate.

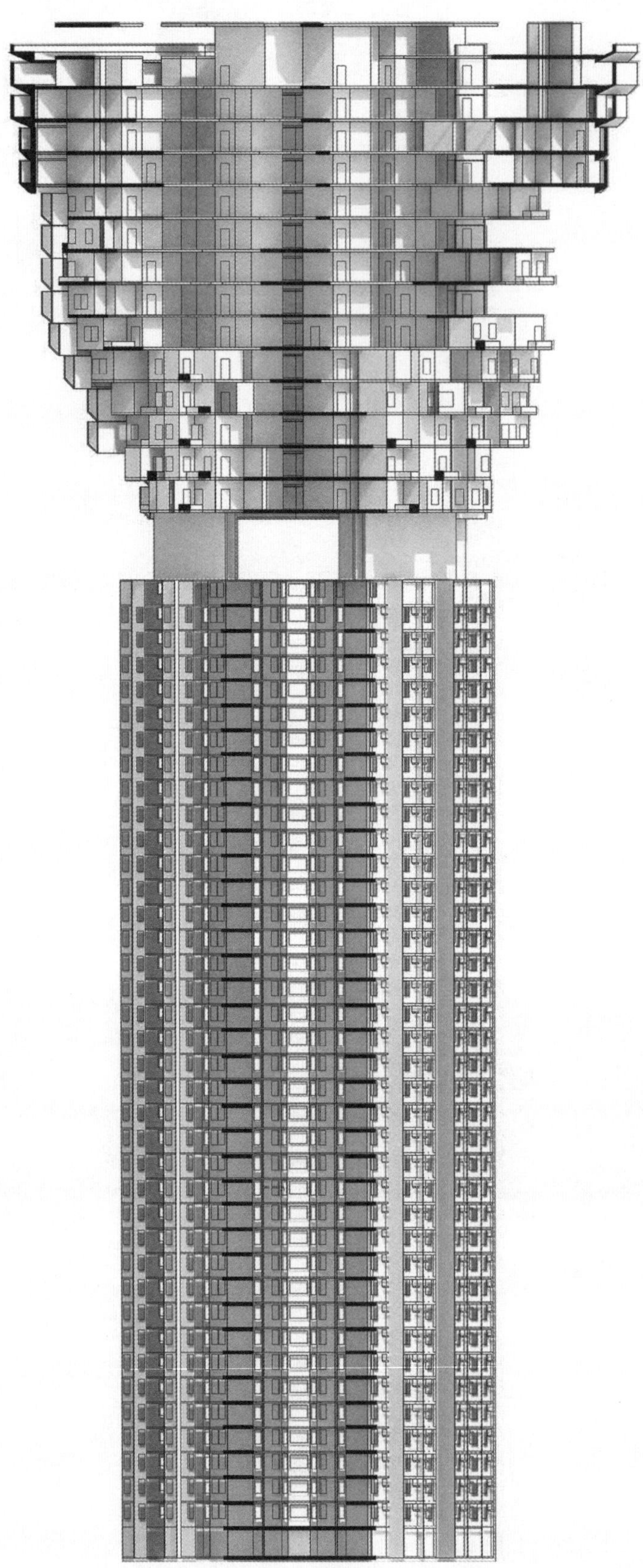

Pair rendering
OPPOSITE Building section

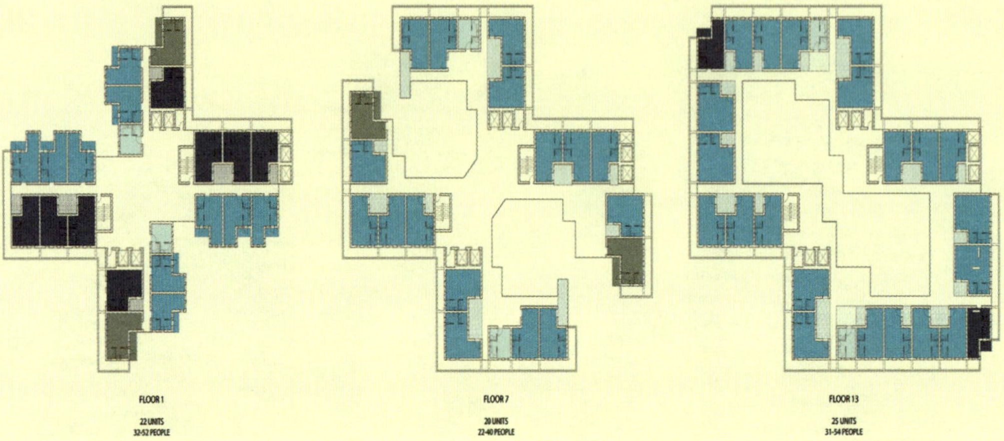

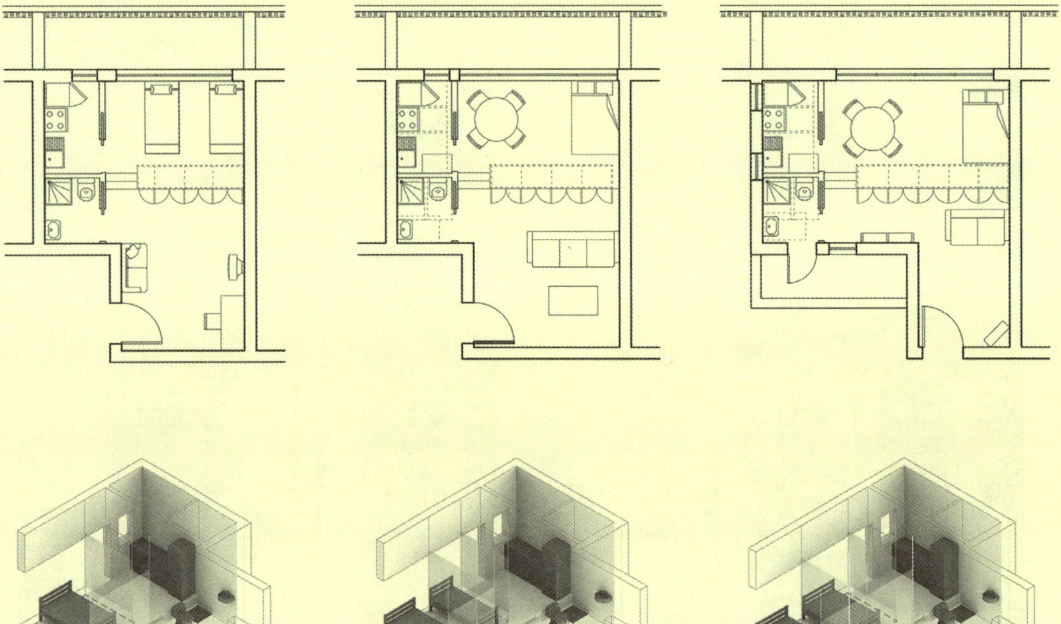

TOP Floor plans
BOTTOM Unit plans and axonometrics
OPPOSITE Model photos

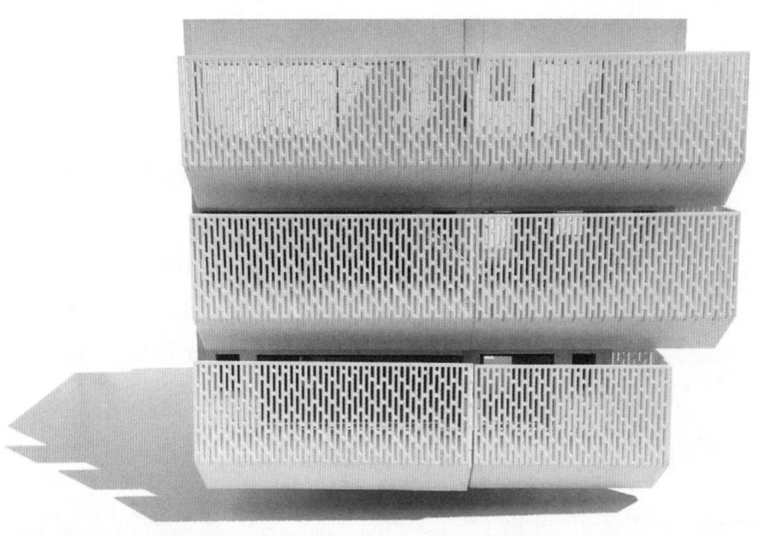

TOP Outside view, looking up
BOTTOM Daylight studies
OPPOSITE Interior view, looking down

THE SEAM

AVA AMIRAHMADI AND CLAUDIA GARRETT HARDEE

This project creates a new world for the inhabitants of the towers. It begins by looking at architecture not from the ground but from thirty-six stories in the air. Through re-origination, the new is stacked on top of the old, and the new façade is stitched to its elder with unique embedded chambers.

Re-origination is achieved through the interdigitation, sidedness, and porosity of the façade. The interdigitation is inspired by the informal roof-sited housing constructions found around Hong Kong. The unit types and solar orientation provide a varied rhythm, creating porosity and transparency as one moves around the towers. This cadence results in sidedness within each block and across the estate as a whole. The façade treatment obfuscates unique chambers, embedded to create an identity within each block. The chambers expand upon the existing trends in amenity spaces in Hong Kong. Exploration and interaction is not prescribed but inherent in the experience of each tower's unique geometry and materiality. These spaces join to connect all of the towers. Materiality and formal geometries are used to selectively heighten or subvert nature and artifice on both the exterior and the interior. The hoped-for sublimity produced by these manipulations will foster a new sense of identity and community across this new datum of the estate.

Exterior perspective of additions

Aerial plan
OPPOSITE Model shot from street view

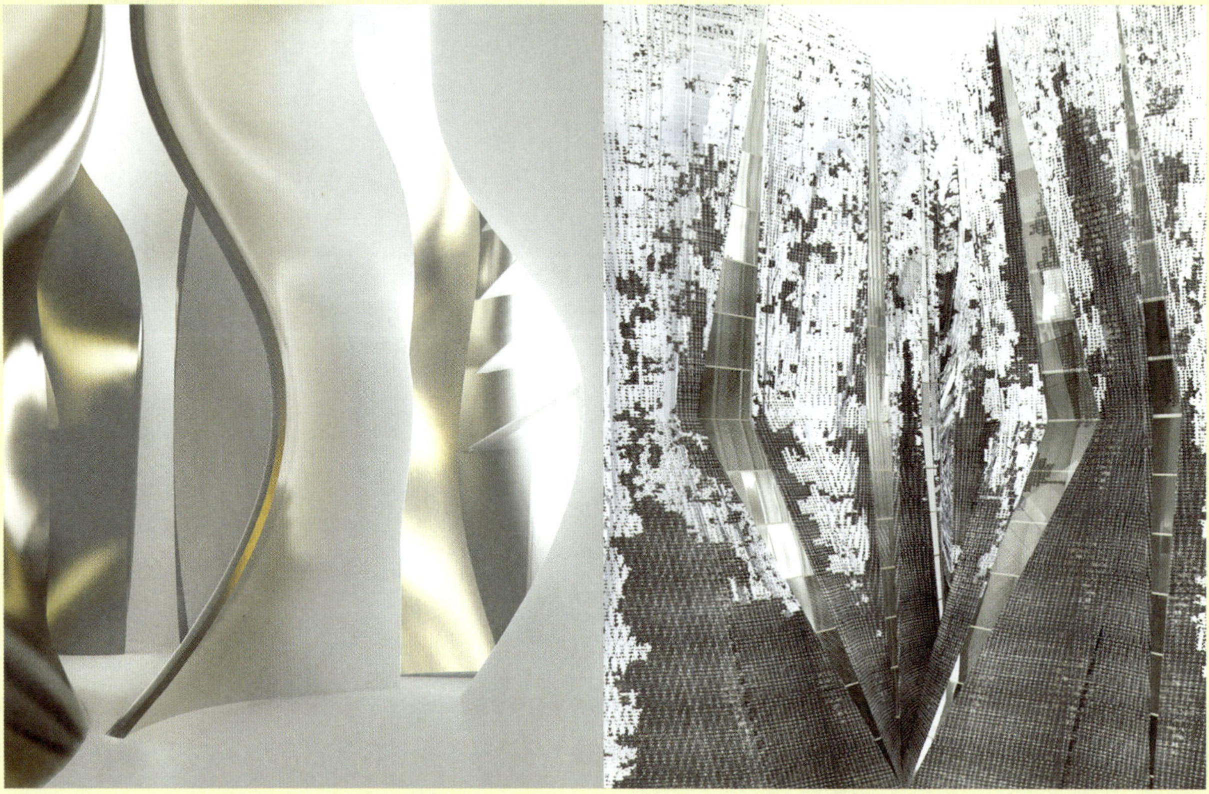

Details of interior chambers

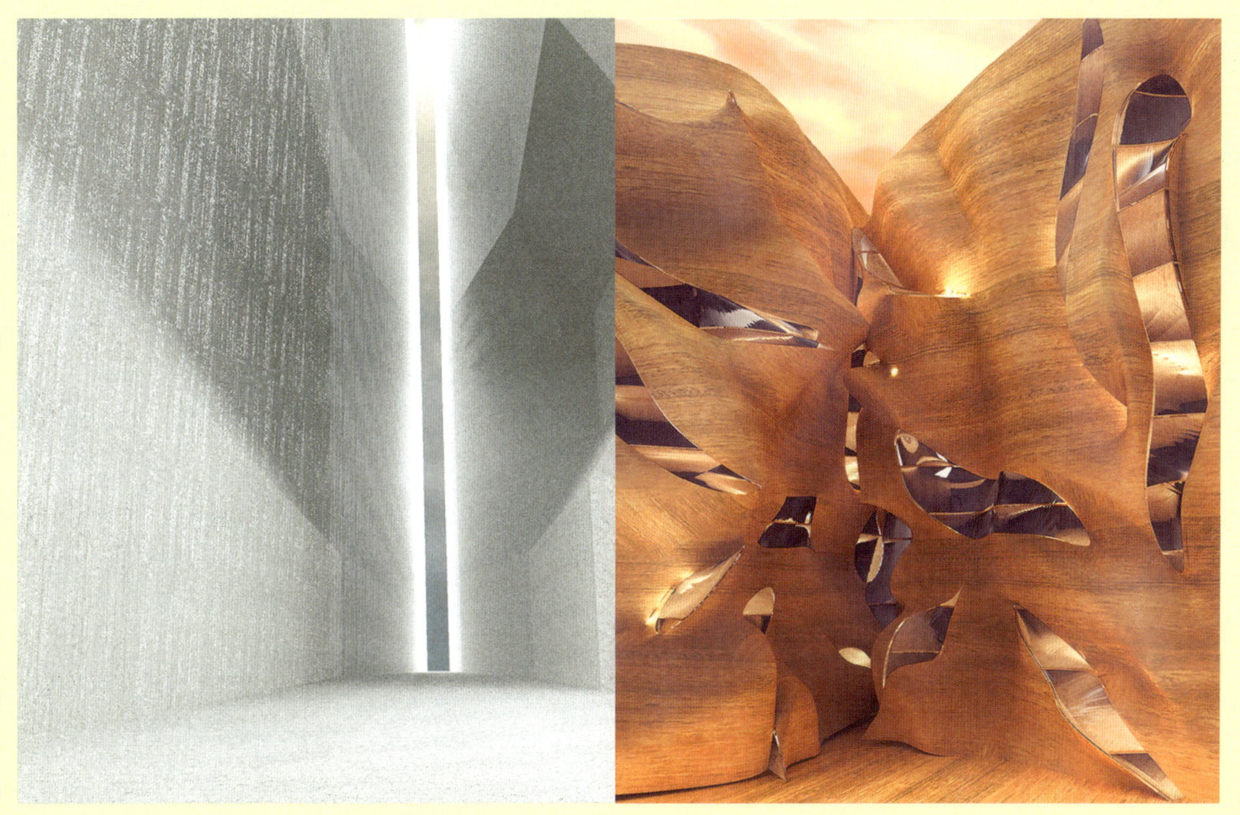

Model shot from street view
OPPOSITE Typical floor plans

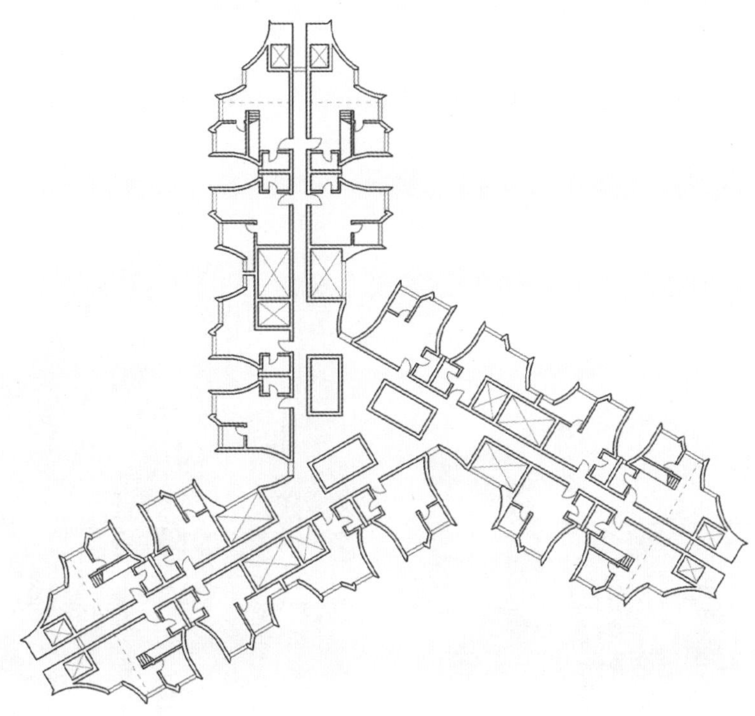

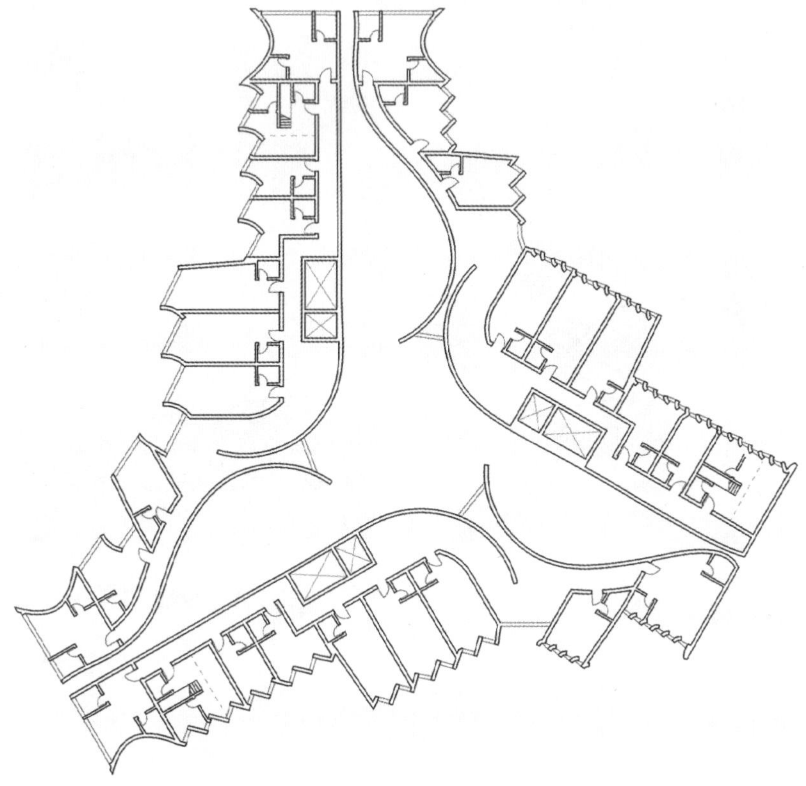

Street view

IMAGE CREDITS

Davidclovers: 3, 4, 7 top, bottom, 8 top, bottom; Herzog and de Meuron: 12 top; Michael Moran/ OTTO: 12 bottom; David Erdman: 17, 19; Rob Cornellison and Jolanda Devalle: 20, 38-39, 40 top, bottom, 41, 42, 43, 44-45, 46 top, bottom, 47; Ilana Simhon and Brittany Olivary: 22, 26-27, 28, 29, 30, 31, 32, 33, 34, 35, 36-37; Francesca Carney, Cecily Ng, Ajin Ryu: 48-49, 50, 51, 52 top, bottom, 53, 54 top, bottom, 55; Ava Amirahmadi and Claudia Garrett Hardee: 56-57, 58, 59, 60-61, 62, 63, 64.